A Day in the Life of a Data Scientist and AI Researcher

Table Of Contents:

Morning Routine

1. *Check and Prioritize Tasks:*

    - *Emails and Slack:* Review messages for any urgent issues or updates from team members or stakeholders.

    - *Task Management:* Update the to-do list based on priorities, deadlines, and ongoing projects.

-

2. *Daily Standup Meeting:*

    - *Team Sync:* Discuss progress on current projects, roadblocks, and next steps. This helps align everyone and plan the day's work effectively.

Core Work Hours

1. *Data Extraction and Preprocessing:*

    - *Data Sources:* Connect to databases or data lakes using tools like SQL or data extraction scripts. For instance, you might use Pandas for data manipulation.

    - *Data Cleaning:* Address missing values, outliers, and inconsistencies. Use techniques in Pandas and NumPy for this.

    - *Feature Engineering:* Create new features from raw data to improve model performance.

2. Exploratory Data Analysis (EDA):
   - Visualization: Use Matplotlib or Seaborn to create plots and understand data distributions and relationships.
   - Insights: Generate reports and share findings using PowerBI.

3. Model Building and Evaluation:
   - Select Algorithms: Choose algorithms based on the problem (e.g., Linear Regression for regression tasks, CatBoost for gradient boosting).
   - Train Models: Implement and train models using frameworks like Scikit-learn, TensorFlow, or PyTorch.
   - Evaluate Performance: Assess model performance using metrics like accuracy, precision, recall, and F1 score.

   o

4. Deployment:

   o *Model Deployment: Deploy models to production. This may involve setting up APIs using Flask or FastAPI, and containerizing the application with Docker.*
   o *Monitor: Ensure that the deployed model is performing as expected and making accurate predictions.*

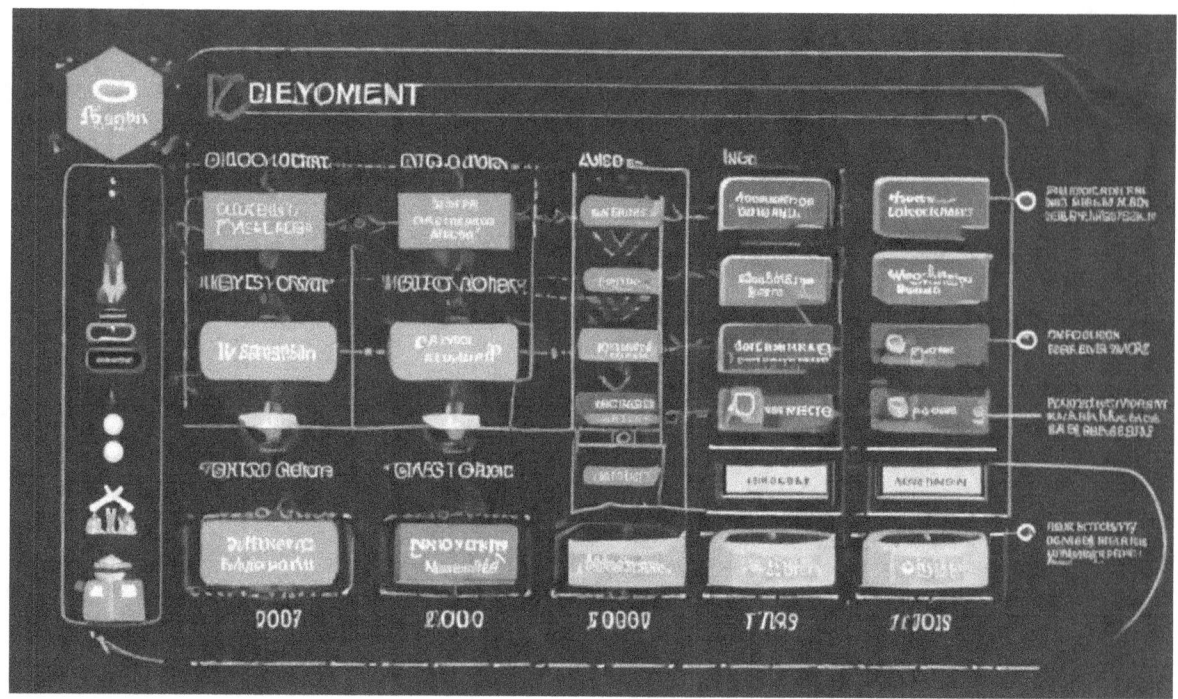

Afternoon Routine

1. *Feedback and Retraining:*

    - *Collect Feedback: Gather performance data and feedback from users or systems.*
    - *Retrain Models: Use new data to update and retrain models, incorporating feedback to improve accuracy.*

2. *Research and Development:*

    - *Stay Updated: Read recent papers and articles on Computer Vision, NLP, AI Agents, Gen AI, and new algorithms to stay current with advancements.*
    - *Experiment: Implement novel ideas or improvements to existing models and techniques.*

3. *Collaborate and Communicate:*

- Team Discussions: Share findings, code, and results with team members. Participate in brainstorming sessions or code reviews.
- Documentation: Document work, including model configurations, data preprocessing steps, and deployment details.

End of Day

1. Wrap-Up:
   - Review Progress: Check completed tasks and update project statuses.
   - Plan for Tomorrow: Set goals and plan tasks for the next day.

2. Learning and Development:
   - New Skills: Allocate time to learn new technologies or improve skills. This might involve working with new tools like Streamlit for creating interactive dashboards or exploring advanced concepts in Deep Learning.

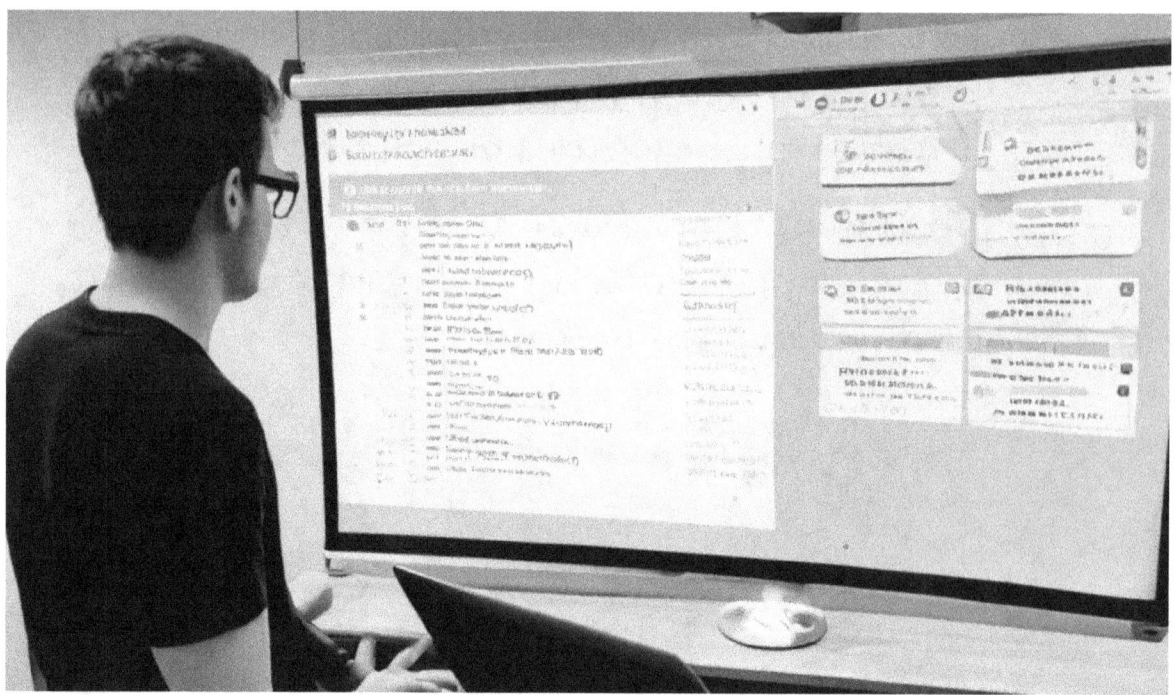

Tech Stack Overview

1. *CRUD Operations:*
    - *Create, Read, Update, Delete: Essential for managing data and models.*

2. *ML Algorithms:*
    - *Linear Regression, CatBoost, Neural Networks: Basic to advanced algorithms for various tasks.*

3. *Frameworks and Libraries:*
    - *TensorFlow, Keras, PyTorch: For building and training deep learning models.*
    - *Scikit-learn: For traditional machine learning algorithms and preprocessing.*
    - *Pandas, NumPy: For data manipulation and numerical operations.*
    - *Matplotlib, PowerBI: For data visualization and reporting.*

- Streamlit: For creating interactive web applications.

4. Advanced Topics:
    - Computer Vision: For image and video analysis.
    - NLP: For natural language processing tasks.
    - AI Agents and Gen AI: For creating intelligent systems and generative models.

5. Deployment and Operations:
    - Flask, Docker: For deploying and managing applications.
    -

Learning Challenges

1. Flask & API Development:
    - Create a Simple API: Develop a basic API using Flask to serve a machine learning model.

2. Docker Imaging:

- Containerize an Application: Use Docker to create a container for a model or application to ensure consistency across environments.

3. End-to-End Projects:
- Build a Complete System: Create a project that covers the entire ML lifecycle, from data collection to model deployment and monitoring.

Simplified Novel-Like Overview

Imagine our data scientist, Alex, starts their day by brewing coffee and checking emails. Their to-do list includes updating a model that predicts customer churn. First, Alex retrieves data from the company's database, cleans it up using Pandas, and visualizes trends with Matplotlib. After analyzing the data, Alex chooses CatBoost for its excellent performance on similar problems.

With the model trained and validated, Alex deploys it using Flask to create an API that the marketing team can use. They then containerize the API with Docker to ensure it runs smoothly in any environment. Throughout the day, Alex participates in team meetings, reviews feedback from the deployed model, and spends some time exploring new techniques in Deep Learning.

By the end of the day, Alex has not only advanced their current projects but also learned a bit about Streamlit and its potential for creating interactive dashboards. They plan to experiment with it tomorrow.

And that's a wrap for Alex's day—a blend of coding, collaboration, learning, and a dash of creativity!

This approach provides a practical, engaging way to understand the daily activities and challenges faced by data scientists and AI researchers, integrating the tech stack and learning challenges effectively.

Learning Challenges in Flask & API Development,

Docker Imaging, and End-to-End Projects

Embarking on learning challenges related to Flask & API Development, Docker Imaging, and End-to-End Projects provides a hands-on approach to mastering critical skills in deploying and managing machine learning models and applications. Each of these challenges addresses a unique aspect of the ML lifecycle, ensuring a comprehensive understanding of both development and operational practices.

1. Flask & API Development

1.1. Challenge: Create a Simple API

Objective: Develop a basic RESTful API using Flask to serve a machine learning model. This exercise will help you understand how to expose a model's predictions via a web interface, allowing for integration with other systems or applications.

Steps to Accomplish This Challenge:

1.1.1. Setup Your Development Environment

1. **Install Flask:**

bash

Code

pip install Flask

2. **Install Flask-RESTful** (optional for easier API creation):

bash

Code

pip install Flask-RESTful

3. **Prepare Your Machine Learning Model:** For simplicity, let's assume you have a pre-trained model (e.g., a scikit-learn model). Save this model using joblib or pickle:

python

Code

import joblib

# Assuming `model` is your trained model
joblib.dump(model, 'model.pkl')

1.1.2. Create the Flask Application

1. **Create a Basic Flask API:**

python

Code

from flask import Flask, request, jsonify
import joblib

```python
import numpy as np

app = Flask(__name__)
model = joblib.load('model.pkl')  # Load the pre-trained model

@app.route('/')
def home():
    return "Welcome to the ML API!"

@app.route('/predict', methods=['POST'])
def predict():
    data = request.get_json()  # Get JSON data from the request
    features = np.array(data['features']).reshape(1, -1)  # Prepare features for prediction
    prediction = model.predict(features)[0]  # Get prediction from the model
    return jsonify({'prediction': prediction})

if __name__ == '__main__':
    app.run(debug=True)
```

2. **Test the API Locally**: Run the Flask application and use tools like Postman or cURL to test the /predict endpoint.

bash

Code

python app.py

Example cURL Request:

bash

Code

```
curl -X POST http://localhost:5000/predict -H "Content-Type: application/json" -d '{"features": [5.1, 3.5, 1.4, 0.2]}'
```

3. **Error Handling and Validation**: Implement error handling and validation to ensure robustness. For example, check if the JSON payload contains the expected fields and handle exceptions.

python

Code

```python
@app.route('/predict', methods=['POST'])
def predict():
    try:
        data = request.get_json()
        features = np.array(data['features']).reshape(1, -1)
        prediction = model.predict(features)[0]
        return jsonify({'prediction': prediction})
    except KeyError:
        return jsonify({'error': 'Missing features in request'}), 400
    except Exception as e:
        return jsonify({'error': str(e)}), 500
```

1.2. Challenge Wrap-Up

- **Testing**: Ensure thorough testing of your API endpoints.
- **Documentation**: Document the API endpoints and their usage.
- **Security**: Consider implementing authentication and validation mechanisms to secure your API.

2. Docker Imaging

2.1. Challenge: Containerize an Application

Objective: Use Docker to create a container for a Flask application or machine learning model to ensure consistency across different environments. This challenge helps you understand containerization principles and deployment practices.

Steps to Accomplish This Challenge:

2.1.1. Install Docker

- **Installation**: Follow Docker's official installation guide for your operating system: Docker Installation Guide

2.1.2. Create a Dockerfile

1. **Create a Dockerfile for Your Flask Application**:

dockerfile

Code

```
# Use an official Python runtime as a parent image
FROM python:3.8-slim

# Set the working directory in the container
```

```
WORKDIR /app

# Copy the requirements file and install dependencies
COPY requirements.txt requirements.txt
RUN pip install --no-cache-dir -r requirements.txt

# Copy the rest of the application code
COPY . .

# Expose port 5000 for the Flask application
EXPOSE 5000

# Define the command to run the application
CMD ["python", "app.py"]
```

    2. **Create a requirements.txt File:** List all the Python packages required by your application.

plaintext

Code

```
Flask==2.0.1
scikit-learn==0.24.2
joblib==1.1.0
```

2.1.3. Build and Run the Docker Container

    1. **Build the Docker Image:**

bash

Code

```
docker build -t my-flask-app .
```

2. **Run the Docker Container:**

bash

Code

```
docker run -p 5000:5000 my-flask-app
```

3. **Verify the Container:** Access the Flask application through http://localhost:5000 to ensure it is working as expected.

2.1.4. Using Docker Compose (Optional)

1. **Create a docker-compose.yml File:**

yaml

Code

```
version: '3'
services:
  web:
    build: .
    ports:
      - "5000:5000"
    environment:
      - FLASK_ENV=production
```

2. **Start Services with Docker Compose:**

bash

Code

```
docker-compose up
```

3. **Stop Services:**

bash

Code

docker-compose down

2.2. Challenge Wrap-Up

- **Container Testing:** Ensure your container runs correctly across different environments.
- **Documentation:** Document the Dockerfile and Docker Compose setup.
- **Best Practices:** Follow best practices for Dockerfile optimization, security, and multi-stage builds.

3. End-to-End Projects

3.1. Challenge: Build a Complete System

Objective: Create a project that covers the entire machine learning lifecycle, from data collection to model deployment and monitoring. This challenge will give you practical experience in building and managing ML systems.

Steps to Accomplish This Challenge:

3.1.1. Define the Project Scope

1. **Project Goal:** Identify the problem you want to solve (e.g., sentiment analysis, image classification).
2. **Dataset:** Acquire or create a dataset relevant to the problem.

3.1.2. Develop the Model

1. **Data Collection and Preprocessing:**

- Collect data from sources (e.g., databases, APIs).
- Clean and preprocess the data.

```python
import pandas as pd
from sklearn.model_selection import train_test_split

# Load data
data = pd.read_csv('data.csv')

# Preprocess data
X = data.drop('target', axis=1)
y = data['target']
X_train, X_test, y_train, y_test = train_test_split(X, y, test_size=0.2)
```

2. **Train the Model:**
   - Select a suitable machine learning algorithm.
   - Train the model on the training data.

```python
from sklearn.ensemble import RandomForestClassifier

model = RandomForestClassifier()
model.fit(X_train, y_train)
```

3. **Evaluate the Model:**
    - Assess the model's performance using evaluation metrics.

python

Code

```
from sklearn.metrics import accuracy_score

predictions = model.predict(X_test)
accuracy = accuracy_score(y_test, predictions)
print(f'Accuracy: {accuracy}')
```

3.1.3. Create the API

1. **Develop a Flask API** (as described in the Flask & API Development section).

3.1.4. Containerize the Application

1. **Create a Dockerfile** (as described in Docker Imaging).
2. **Build and Run the Docker Container** (as described in Docker Imaging).

3.1.5. Deploy and Monitor

1. **Deployment:**
    - Deploy your Docker container to a cloud provider or on-premises server.
    - Set up a reverse proxy (e.g., Nginx) if needed.
2. **Monitoring:**
    - Implement logging to track application performance and errors.

- Use monitoring tools to observe system metrics and resource usage.

Example Logging Configuration in Flask:

python

Code

```python
import logging
from logging.handlers import RotatingFileHandler

handler = RotatingFileHandler('app.log', maxBytes=10000, backupCount=1)
handler.setLevel(logging.INFO)
app.logger.addHandler(handler)
```

3. **Scaling**:
    - Scale your application horizontally by running multiple instances of your Docker container.
    - Use orchestration tools like Kubernetes for managing multiple containers.

3.2. Challenge Wrap-Up

- **End-to-End Integration**: Ensure that all components (data pipeline, model, API, containerization) work together seamlessly.
- **Documentation**: Document the entire project, including setup instructions, usage, and configuration.
- **Testing and Validation**: Perform thorough testing and validation across all stages of the project.

Conclusion

Completing these learning challenges provides a comprehensive understanding of deploying and managing machine learning applications. Mastering Flask for API development, Docker for containerization, and end-to-end project development equips you with the skills needed to transition from model development to production environments successfully. By tackling these challenges, you'll gain practical experience in building robust, scalable, and maintainable systems, which are crucial for any data scientist or machine learning engineer.

A Day in the Life of a Data Scientist: Alex's Journey Through Data Science, Deployment, and Continuous Learning

Chapter 1: Morning Routine and Project Kickoff

1.1. The Day Begins

The first rays of morning sun peek through the curtains as Alex, a seasoned data scientist, starts their day with a comforting ritual: brewing a fresh cup of coffee. With the rich aroma of coffee filling the room, Alex sits down at their desk, ready to tackle the tasks of the day. They open their laptop, check their emails, and review their to-do list.

1.2. Setting the Stage

Today's focus is a critical project: updating a predictive model for customer churn. This model is vital for the company's marketing strategy, helping to identify customers who are likely to stop using the service. The aim is to improve the model's accuracy and make it more robust against new patterns in the data.

Chapter 2: Data Retrieval and Preparation

2.1. Data Extraction

Alex starts by retrieving the latest data from the company's database. They use SQL queries to pull relevant datasets, which include customer interactions, purchase history, and engagement metrics. The extracted data is saved in a CSV file for further processing.

2.2. Cleaning the Data

With the raw data in hand, Alex's first task is to clean it. They open a Python notebook and use Pandas, a powerful data manipulation library, to handle this. Alex performs several steps:

- **Removing Duplicates**: They eliminate any duplicate entries to ensure the dataset's integrity.
- **Handling Missing Values**: Missing values are either imputed using statistical methods or dropped if too numerous.
- **Data Transformation**: Columns are converted to appropriate data types, and categorical variables are encoded.

python

Code

```python
import pandas as pd

# Load the data
data = pd.read_csv('customer_data.csv')

# Remove duplicates
data = data.drop_duplicates()
```

```python
# Handle missing values
data = data.fillna(method='ffill')

# Convert categorical variables
data['gender'] = data['gender'].astype('category').cat.codes
```

2.3. Exploratory Data Analysis

Next, Alex uses Matplotlib to visualize trends and relationships in the data. They create several plots:

- **Histograms**: To understand the distribution of numerical features.
- **Scatter Plots**: To identify relationships between features.
- **Box Plots**: To detect outliers.

python

Code

```python
import matplotlib.pyplot as plt

# Histogram of customer age
plt.hist(data['age'], bins=20)
plt.title('Distribution of Customer Age')
plt.xlabel('Age')
plt.ylabel('Frequency')
plt.show()
```

```
# Scatter plot of engagement vs. churn
plt.scatter(data['engagement_score'], data['churn'])
plt.title('Engagement vs. Churn')
plt.xlabel('Engagement Score')
plt.ylabel('Churn')
plt.show()
```

These visualizations help Alex to spot trends, correlations, and anomalies in the data, guiding the subsequent steps in model development.

Chapter 3: Model Development and Training

3.1. Choosing the Algorithm

After analyzing the data, Alex decides to use CatBoost, a gradient boosting library known for its performance with categorical features. CatBoost's ability to handle categorical data efficiently and its robustness against overfitting make it a suitable choice for this problem.

3.2. Training the Model

Alex splits the data into training and testing sets and begins the training process. They use CatBoost's API to fit the model on the training data and evaluate its performance on the test set.

python

Code

```
from catboost import CatBoostClassifier

# Split data
```

```python
from sklearn.model_selection import train_test_split
X = data.drop('churn', axis=1)
y = data['churn']
X_train, X_test, y_train, y_test = train_test_split(X, y, test_size=0.2)

# Initialize and train the CatBoost model
model = CatBoostClassifier(iterations=1000, depth=6, learning_rate=0.1)
model.fit(X_train, y_train)

# Evaluate the model
accuracy = model.score(X_test, y_test)
print(f'Model Accuracy: {accuracy}')
```

3.3. Model Validation

Alex evaluates the model's performance using various metrics like accuracy, precision, recall, and F1 score. They also plot the ROC curve to assess the model's ability to distinguish between classes.

python

Code

```python
from sklearn.metrics import classification_report, roc_curve

# Predictions
y_pred = model.predict(X_test)
```

```python
# Classification report
print(classification_report(y_test, y_pred))

# ROC Curve
fpr, tpr, _ = roc_curve(y_test, model.predict_proba(X_test)[:,1])
plt.plot(fpr, tpr)
plt.title('ROC Curve')
plt.xlabel('False Positive Rate')
plt.ylabel('True Positive Rate')
plt.show()
```

Chapter 4: Deploying the Model

4.1. Creating the API with Flask

With the model trained and validated, Alex proceeds to deploy it so that the marketing team can use it. They choose Flask, a lightweight web framework, to create a RESTful API. This API will serve predictions based on new data sent to it.

Flask API Code:

python

Code

```python
from flask import Flask, request, jsonify
import joblib
import numpy as np
```

```python
app = Flask(__name__)
model = joblib.load('model.pkl')  # Load the trained model


@app.route('/')
def home():
    return "Welcome to the Churn Prediction API!"


@app.route('/predict', methods=['POST'])
def predict():
    data = request.get_json()
    features = np.array(data['features']).reshape(1, -1)
    prediction = model.predict(features)[0]
    return jsonify({'prediction': prediction})


if __name__ == '__main__':
    app.run(debug=True)
```

4.2. Containerizing the Application with Docker

To ensure the Flask API runs consistently across different environments, Alex containerizes it using Docker. They create a Dockerfile to define the container image.

Dockerfile:

dockerfile

Code

```
FROM python:3.8-slim

WORKDIR /app

COPY requirements.txt requirements.txt
RUN pip install --no-cache-dir -r requirements.txt

COPY . .

EXPOSE 5000
CMD ["python", "app.py"]
```

Alex builds the Docker image and runs it to test the deployment.

bash

Code

```
docker build -t churn-prediction-api .
docker run -p 5000:5000 churn-prediction-api
```

4.3. Testing and Validation

Alex tests the API endpoints using tools like Postman to ensure that predictions are served correctly. They also check for any potential security vulnerabilities and performance issues.

Chapter 5: Collaboration and Continuous Learning

5.1. Team Meetings

Throughout the day, Alex participates in team meetings to discuss project progress, share findings, and gather feedback. They review how the deployed model is performing and consider suggestions for further improvements.

5.2. Code Reviews

Alex engages in code reviews, providing and receiving feedback on code quality, efficiency, and best practices. This collaboration helps in maintaining high standards and fostering a learning environment.

5.3. Exploring New Techniques

Curiosity drives Alex to explore new technologies and techniques. Today, they take some time to learn about Streamlit, a framework for creating interactive web applications. Streamlit offers an easy way to build data-driven dashboards and visualization tools.

Streamlit Exploration: Alex follows tutorials to understand how to use Streamlit for creating interactive applications. They experiment with creating a simple dashboard to visualize model predictions and performance metrics.

python

Code

```python
import streamlit as st
import pandas as pd


st.title('Customer Churn Prediction Dashboard')
```

```
uploaded_file = st.file_uploader("Upload your data", type="csv")
if uploaded_file is not None:
    data = pd.read_csv(uploaded_file)
    st.write(data.head())
    # Further exploration and visualization
```

5.4. Planning for Tomorrow

Before wrapping up for the day, Alex reflects on their accomplishments and plans for tomorrow. They note to dive deeper into Streamlit and consider integrating it with their Flask API for enhanced interactive capabilities.

Chapter 6: Wrapping Up the Day

6.1. End-of-Day Review

As the day comes to a close, Alex reviews the tasks completed and updates the project statuses. They ensure that all code is properly documented, and any insights or issues from the day are noted.

6.2. Learning and Development

Alex allocates time to reflect on the new skills acquired and set goals for further learning. They plan to explore advanced topics in Deep Learning and continue experimenting with Streamlit.

6.3. Relaxation and Reflection

With the day's work done, Alex enjoys a well-deserved break. They reflect on the challenges faced and the progress made, feeling accomplished and eager to tackle new tasks in the future.

Conclusion

Alex's day as a data scientist is a blend of coding, collaboration, and continuous learning. From cleaning and analyzing data to deploying models and exploring new tools, each task contributes to their growth and the success of their projects. This journey illustrates the dynamic and multifaceted nature of a data scientist's role, combining technical skills with creativity and teamwork.

Glossary

1. **Data Science**: The field that combines statistical analysis, machine learning, and data visualization to extract insights and inform decision-making from data.

2. **CatBoost**: A gradient boosting library developed by Yandex that is particularly effective with categorical features. It is used for building predictive models and is known for its high performance and ease of use.

3. **Flask API**: A lightweight web framework in Python used to create web applications and RESTful APIs. It allows developers to build web services that can serve machine learning model predictions to clients.

4. **Docker**: A platform for developing, shipping, and running applications in containers. Docker ensures that applications run consistently across different environments by packaging them with their dependencies.

5. **Pandas**: A Python library for data manipulation and analysis. It provides data structures like DataFrames for handling and analyzing structured data efficiently.

6. **Streamlit**: An open-source framework for creating interactive web applications for data science projects. It allows users to build dashboards and visualizations with minimal code.

7. **Customer Churn**: The phenomenon where customers stop using a company's products or services. Predictive models for churn aim to identify customers who are likely to leave, enabling targeted retention strategies.

References

1. **Data Science:**
   - **"Data Science for Business"** by Foster Provost and Tom Fawcett: A comprehensive guide on how data science can be used for business decision-making.
   - [Data Science Overview - Wikipedia](#)

2. **CatBoost:**
   - **Official CatBoost Documentation:** CatBoost Documentation
   - **"CatBoost: Gradient Boosting with Categorical Features Support"**: [CatBoost Paper](#)

3. **Flask API:**
   - **Official Flask Documentation:** Flask Documentation
   - **"Flask Web Development"** by Miguel Grinberg: A book that provides a comprehensive guide to building web applications with Flask.

4. **Docker:**
   - **Official Docker Documentation:** Docker Documentation
   - **"Docker Deep Dive"** by Nigel Poulton: A detailed book on Docker, covering both basic and advanced topics.

5. **Pandas:**
   - **Official Pandas Documentation:** Pandas Documentation
   - **"Python for Data Analysis"** by Wes McKinney: A foundational book by the creator of Pandas, covering data analysis techniques and best practices.

6. **Streamlit:**
   - **Official Streamlit Documentation:** Streamlit Documentation
   - **"Streamlit for Data Science"**: A practical guide for building interactive applications with Streamlit. Streamlit Official Blog

7. **Customer Churn:**
   - **"Customer Churn Prediction: Methods and Applications"**: An overview of various methods for predicting customer churn. ResearchGate Paper
   - **"Practical Guide to Customer Churn Prediction"**: Towards Data Science Article

These references cover the fundamental concepts, tools, and best practices involved in data science and machine learning model deployment.

Morning Routine of a Data Scientist and AI Researcher

The morning routine of a data scientist and AI researcher is a crucial phase that sets the tone for the day's productivity. It involves checking and prioritizing tasks, staying in sync with the team, and planning effectively to address both immediate and long-term objectives. Here's an in-depth exploration of these morning activities:

1. Check and Prioritize Tasks

a. Emails and Slack

i. Reviewing Messages: When starting the day, the first task is to dive into the influx of emails and Slack messages that have accumulated overnight. For a data scientist, this often involves scanning for:

- **Urgent Issues:** These could include alerts about system failures, data anomalies, or critical bugs in the deployed models. Immediate attention might be required to address these issues to minimize downtime and impact.

- **Updates from Team Members:** Updates might involve progress on shared projects, completed tasks, or changes that affect collaborative work. Keeping up-to-date with these changes is essential for maintaining project alignment.

- **Stakeholder Communication:** Messages from stakeholders may include feedback on deliverables, requests for additional analyses, or changes in project scope. Understanding and addressing these requests is crucial for meeting stakeholder expectations and ensuring project success.

ii. Triaging Priorities: Once the initial review is complete, the next step is to triage the tasks based on urgency and importance. This involves:

- **Sorting Tasks:** Categorize tasks into immediate, high-priority, and low-priority. Immediate tasks are those that require prompt action to avoid disruptions. High-priority tasks are critical but may not need immediate action. Low-priority tasks are important but can be scheduled for later.

- **Setting Priorities:** Establishing a clear priority order helps in focusing on what matters most. For instance, if a critical bug is reported in a model, fixing it would take precedence over exploring new algorithms or preparing for a presentation.

- **Delegating Tasks:** For tasks that can be handled by team members, delegation is key. Assigning tasks based on team members' expertise and current workload helps in balancing the load and leveraging each member's strengths.

b. Task Management

i. **Updating the To-Do List:** A well-organized to-do list is fundamental for effective task management. This involves:

- **Reviewing Previous Day's Accomplishments:** Assess what was completed the previous day and note any pending tasks that need to be carried forward.

- **Adding New Tasks:** Include new tasks that have emerged from recent communications or project developments. This could involve setting up a new model experiment, preparing for a client meeting, or addressing a newly identified data quality issue.

- **Prioritizing Tasks:** Reevaluate and adjust the priority of tasks based on new information. For instance, a newly received urgent request from a stakeholder might necessitate shifting priorities.

- **Scheduling Tasks:** Allocate specific time blocks for each task to ensure balanced progress throughout the day. This might involve setting aside time for focused work, meetings, and unexpected issues.

ii. Time Management: Effective time management is crucial for balancing various responsibilities. Techniques include:

- *Time Blocking:* Assign specific time blocks for different types of work, such as data analysis, model development, and meetings. This helps in maintaining focus and preventing task overlap.
- *Setting Goals:* Establish clear, achievable goals for the day. For instance, completing the initial training of a new model or finalizing a data report.
- *Avoiding Distractions:* Implement strategies to minimize interruptions during focused work periods. This could involve using tools like "Do Not Disturb" mode or creating a distraction-free workspace.

2. Daily Standup Meeting

a. Team Sync

i. Preparing for the Meeting: Preparation is key to a productive standup meeting. This involves:

- *Reviewing Agenda:* Familiarize yourself with the meeting agenda, which typically includes updates on project progress, identification of roadblocks, and planning next steps.
- *Compiling Updates:* Gather and organize updates on your tasks, including progress made, any issues encountered, and upcoming milestones.

- *Identifying Key Points:* Highlight any critical issues or dependencies that need to be addressed in the meeting.

ii. Participating in the Meeting: The daily standup meeting is a short, focused meeting where team members share updates and discuss challenges. Participation includes:

- *Providing Updates:* Share your progress on assigned tasks, including what was completed since the last meeting and what is planned for the day. This helps in keeping the team informed and aligned.

- *Discussing Roadblocks:* Highlight any obstacles or issues that are impeding progress. This could involve technical challenges, data issues, or dependencies on other team members.

- *Planning Next Steps:* Collaborate with the team to plan the next steps, set priorities, and allocate resources. This ensures that everyone is on the same page and can work together effectively.

iii. Addressing Team Dynamics: Effective standup meetings foster team collaboration and communication. This involves:

- *Encouraging Participation:* Ensure that all team members have the opportunity to contribute and voice any concerns or updates.

- *Maintaining Focus:* Keep the meeting focused on key points to avoid unnecessary discussions and ensure that it remains productive.

- *Following Up:* Post-meeting, follow up on any action items or decisions made during the meeting. This *helps in ensuring that agreed-upon steps are implemented and progress is tracked.*

iv. Leveraging Standup Meetings for Continuous Improvement: Standup meetings provide an opportunity for continuous improvement. This includes:

- **Reviewing Meeting Effectiveness:** Assess the effectiveness of the meeting format and make adjustments as needed to improve efficiency and relevance.

- **Seeking Feedback:** Gather feedback from team members on how the meetings can be improved. This could involve adjusting the frequency, format, or agenda of the meetings.

- **Implementing Best Practices:** Adopt best practices for standup meetings, such as keeping them concise, focusing on actionable items, and encouraging open communication.

Conclusion

The morning routine of a data scientist and AI researcher is a critical phase that sets the stage for a productive day. Checking and prioritizing tasks ensures that urgent issues are addressed, and tasks are organized effectively. Participating in the daily standup meeting facilitates team synchronization, helps in identifying and overcoming roadblocks, and plans the next steps for collaborative success. By managing tasks efficiently and engaging in effective team communication, data scientists and AI researchers can navigate their complex and dynamic work environment with greater ease and effectiveness.

Let's get into dialogues:

The Dawn of Data: A Day in

the Life of Alex the Data Scientist

Setting: A modern office space with an open-plan layout. The morning sun filters through large windows, casting a warm glow on the desks. Alex, the data scientist, sits at their workstation, surrounded by multiple screens displaying code, charts, and emails.

Scene 1: The Morning Ritual

Alex: [Yawning and stretching] "Another day, another set of challenges. Let's see what's on the agenda today."

Alex's Digital Assistant (ADA): [Voice over] "Good morning, Alex. Here's your morning briefing: You have 32 new emails and 14 Slack messages. You're also scheduled for a standup meeting in 30 minutes. Should I pull up your to-do list?"

Alex: [Rubbing eyes] "Yes, please. And can you summarize the emails and Slack messages for me?"

ADA: [Voice over] "Certainly. Your emails include three critical alerts from the monitoring system, two follow-up messages from stakeholders, and a couple of administrative notices. Slack messages involve updates from your team members and a new issue reported in the data pipeline."

Alex: [Nodding] "Got it. Let's start with the emails. Open the critical alerts first."

Alex clicks on the first email, reading the details of a system alert indicating a potential issue with one of the deployed models.

Alex: [Frowning] "Looks like the model's performance metrics have dropped. I'll need to dive into this ASAP. What's next?"

ADA: [Voice over] "The next critical alert involves an anomaly in the data ingestion process. It seems like we're missing some data points."

Alex: [Typing furiously] "I'll need to investigate that too. I'll make a note to check the data pipeline logs and see what's going wrong. Let's move on to the Slack messages."

Alex navigates to Slack and starts reviewing the messages.

Alex: [Reading aloud] "Team member A is having trouble with the feature extraction code. Team member B has completed the data preprocessing script and is ready for the next step. And, oh, there's a new issue reported with the model evaluation metrics."

ADA: [Voice over] "Shall I update your to-do list with these tasks?"

Alex: [Determined] "Yes, please. Add investigating the model performance drop, checking the data pipeline, and assisting team member A with the feature extraction code."

ADA: [Voice over] "Adding these tasks now. Your to-do list has been updated. Is there anything else you need?"

Alex: [Glancing at the clock] "Not right now. I need to prepare for the standup meeting. Can you pull up the agenda for me?"

ADA: [Voice over] "Certainly. The agenda includes a review of progress on current projects, discussion of roadblocks, and planning the next steps. You'll need to provide updates on your tasks and address any issues you're facing."

Alex: [Smiling] "Perfect. Let's get ready for the meeting."

Scene 2: The Standup Meeting

Setting: A conference room with a large table and several chairs. The team members gather around, each with a laptop open and notes in hand.

Team Lead (Sara): "Good morning, everyone. Let's get started with our daily standup. Alex, would you like to begin?"

Alex: [Standing up] "Sure. Good morning, everyone. Here's what I've been working on. We've had a drop in model performance that I need to investigate. Also, there's a data ingestion issue that might be affecting our data quality."

Sara: [Nodding] "Thanks for the update, Alex. Any roadblocks you're facing?"

Alex: [Pausing] "Yes, actually. Team member A is having trouble with the feature extraction code. I'll be helping them out. And there's an issue with the model evaluation metrics that I need to address."

Sara: [Taking notes] "Got it. Let's make sure we prioritize these issues. How about the rest of the team?"

Team Member A (Jordan): "I'm stuck on the feature extraction. I'm not sure if the problem is with the code or the data."

Alex: [Turning to Jordan] "Let's sync up after the meeting. I'll help you troubleshoot the code."

Team Member B (Riley): "I've completed the data preprocessing script. Ready to move on to the next step."

Sara: [Encouragingly] "Great. Riley, you can start integrating the new features into the model. Any other updates or issues?"

Team Member C (Sam): "I've been reviewing the model evaluation metrics. It seems like there's a discrepancy in the results."

Alex: [Addressing Sam] "I'll take a look at that too. It might be related to the issues we're seeing with the model."

Sara: [Wrapping up] "Okay, let's make sure we tackle these tasks. Alex, focus on investigating the model and data pipeline issues first. Jordan, sync up with Alex. Riley, proceed with the integration, and Sam, keep us updated on the metrics. Anything else before we wrap up?"

Team: [Shaking heads] "Nope."

Sara: "Alright, let's get to work. Thanks, everyone!"

Scene 3: Task Management and Prioritization

Setting: Alex's workstation. Alex is now focused on their computer, organizing tasks and planning the day.

Alex: [Opening the to-do list] "Okay, let's break this down. First, I need to address the model performance drop. I'll start by checking the logs and recent changes."

ADA: [Voice over] "Would you like me to pull up the model logs and recent deployment changes?"

Alex: [Nodding] "Yes, please. And while that's loading, I'll look into the data pipeline issue."

Alex navigates to the data pipeline monitoring tool and starts reviewing the recent logs.

Alex: [Muttering to self] "There's definitely a data gap here. It looks like the ingestion process failed due to a timeout error."

ADA: [Voice over] "The model logs and deployment changes are now available. The recent changes include an update to the feature extraction module and a configuration adjustment."

Alex: [Reviewing logs] "The performance drop coincides with the feature extraction update. It might be causing issues. I'll need to compare the old and new feature sets."

Alex opens the feature extraction code and starts comparing.

Alex: [Focused] "Let's see... The new feature set includes additional features, but there might be some inconsistencies."

ADA: [Voice over] "Shall I set up a meeting with Jordan to discuss the feature extraction code?"

Alex: [Typing] "Yes, please. Arrange a meeting for later today. I'll also need to draft a plan for investigating the model evaluation metrics."

Alex switches to drafting a plan for the model evaluation issue.

Alex: [Writing] "I'll start by reviewing the evaluation script and comparing it with the expected results. If needed, I'll consult with Sam."

ADA: [Voice over] "The meeting with Jordan is scheduled for 2 PM. Is there anything else you need?"

Alex: [Leaning back] "No, that's it for now. I'll focus on these tasks and update the team on my progress."

Scene 4: Addressing Issues and Collaborating

Setting: Alex is now meeting with Jordan at a collaborative workspace.

Jordan: "Thanks for meeting with me, Alex. I'm really stuck on this feature extraction code. I'm not sure if it's a data issue or something in the code."

Alex: [Reviewing the code] "Let's take a look. Can you walk me through what you've implemented?"

Jordan: [Pointing at the screen] "Here's where I'm extracting features from the dataset. I've added a few new features, but the results aren't matching the expected output."

Alex: [Examining the code] "I see. It might be an issue with how the new features are being processed. Let's check the data to ensure it aligns with the feature extraction logic."

Alex and Jordan review the dataset and feature extraction logic.

Jordan: "I think I see the issue now. There's a mismatch in how we're handling categorical variables."

Alex: [Nodding] "Exactly. Let's update the code to handle these variables correctly and re-run the feature extraction."

Jordan: "Got it. I'll make the changes and test it again."

Alex: "Great. I'll follow up with you later to review the results."

Later in the day, Alex is working on the model evaluation metrics with Sam.

Sam: "I've been analyzing the discrepancies in the model evaluation. It seems like the evaluation script isn't accounting for the new features correctly."

Alex: [Reviewing the script] "Let's compare it with the previous version. We might need to update the evaluation logic to reflect the changes in the feature set."

Sam: "I'll make the necessary adjustments and re-evaluate the model."

Alex: "Perfect. Keep me updated on your progress."

Scene 5: Reflection and Planning

Setting: Alex's workstation, late afternoon. Alex is reviewing progress and planning the next steps.

Alex: [Checking progress] "The feature extraction issue seems to be resolved. Jordan updated the code, and the results are now aligning with expectations."

ADA: [Voice over] "The model evaluation issue is still being worked on. Sam is adjusting the evaluation script and will provide an update soon."

Alex: [Nodding] "Good. I'll check in with Sam later. For now, let's review the feedback from the standup meeting and plan for tomorrow."

Alex reviews the standup notes and updates the to-do list.

Alex: [Writing] "For tomorrow, I need to follow up on the model performance investigation and check the results from the updated evaluation script."

ADA: [Voice over] "Shall I schedule time for these tasks tomorrow?"

Alex: [Smiling] "Yes, please. Also, schedule a brief meeting with the team to review the progress and address any new issues."

ADA: [Voice over] "Scheduling now. Is there anything else?"

Alex: [Leaning back] "No, that's all for today. Let's wrap things up."

ADA: [Voice over] "Have a great evening, Alex."

Alex shuts down the workstation and prepares to leave the office, reflecting on a productive day of tackling challenges and collaborating with the team.

Conclusion

In this detailed narrative, we explored the morning routine of a data scientist and AI researcher through a dialogue format. From checking and prioritizing tasks to participating in standup meetings and addressing issues, we delved into the daily activities that drive productivity and ensure successful project outcomes. The dialogue provided an engaging and immersive look at the intricacies of managing tasks, collaborating with team members, and navigating the complex world of data science and AI research.

By following Alex's journey, readers gained insight into the critical aspects of the profession and the essential skills required to excel in this dynamic field.

Core Work Hours of a Data Scientist and AI Researcher

The core work hours of a data scientist and AI researcher involve a series of intricate and methodical steps focused on data extraction, preprocessing, and feature engineering. These processes are fundamental for ensuring that data is accurate, usable, and valuable for model building and analysis. Let's delve deeply into each aspect of this work, exploring the tools, techniques, and best practices employed.

---

1. Data Extraction and Preprocessing

a. Data Extraction

Setting: Alex's workspace, filled with multiple monitors displaying various data sources and tools. Alex is ready to begin the data extraction process.

Alex: [Sipping coffee] "Alright, it's time to pull the data for today's analysis. First, I need to connect to our databases and extract the required datasets."

ADA (Alex's Digital Assistant): [Voice over] "Good morning, Alex. The data sources for today include our customer database, transaction logs, and external market data. Should I initiate the connections?"

Alex: [Typing] "Yes, please. Connect to the SQL database for customer data and load the transaction logs from the data lake. We'll also need to fetch the market data via the API."

ADA: [Voice over] "Connecting now. I'm initiating the SQL queries for the customer database and setting up the API request for the market data."

As ADA works in the background, Alex prepares the data extraction scripts.

Alex: [Writing code] "I'll use SQL to query our customer database. Let's retrieve the relevant columns: customer_id, age, gender, and purchase_history."

Alex writes a SQL query:

sql

Code

```sql
SELECT customer_id, age, gender, purchase_history
FROM customers
WHERE registration_date BETWEEN '2023-01-01' AND '2023-12-31';
```

Alex: [Reviewing the results] "Perfect. The query has been executed, and we've got the customer data. Now, let's move on to the transaction logs."

For the data lake, Alex writes a Python script to load the data:

python

Code

```python
import pandas as pd

# Load transaction logs from data lake
transaction_logs = pd.read_csv('s3://data-lake/transaction_logs.csv')
```

Alex: [Nodding] "The transaction logs are loaded. Next, we'll need to pull the market data from the API."

Alex writes a script to fetch market data:

python

Code

import requests

API request for market data

response = requests.get('https://api.marketdata.com/v1/market_data')

market_data = response.json()

ADA: [Voice over] "Data extraction is complete. You have customer data, transaction logs, and market data ready for preprocessing."

---

b. Data Cleaning

Setting: Alex's workstation, now focusing on preprocessing the extracted data. The screen shows a Jupyter notebook with the initial data loaded.

Alex: [Examining data] "The next step is data cleaning. I need to address missing values, outliers, and inconsistencies."

ADA: [Voice over] "The customer data contains some missing values and potential outliers. The transaction logs have a few inconsistencies in timestamps, and the market data has some outlier values."

Alex begins with the customer data using Pandas:

python

Code

```python
import pandas as pd
import numpy as np

# Load customer data into a DataFrame
customer_data = pd.read_sql_query('SELECT * FROM customers', conn)

# Checking for missing values
print(customer_data.isnull().sum())
```

Alex: [Reviewing the output] "We have missing values in the age and purchase_history columns. Let's handle these."

Alex decides on the strategy for handling missing values:

- **For Numerical Columns:** Use the median value to fill in missing ages.
- **For Categorical Columns:** Fill missing purchase history with a placeholder like 'Unknown'.

python

Code

```python
# Fill missing values in numerical column with median
customer_data['age'].fillna(customer_data['age'].median(), inplace=True)
```

```python
# Fill missing values in categorical column with placeholder
customer_data['purchase_history'].fillna('Unknown', inplace=True)
```

Alex: [Typing] "Now, let's check for outliers. I'll use a boxplot to visualize the age distribution."

python

Code

```python
import matplotlib.pyplot as plt

# Boxplot for age distribution
plt.boxplot(customer_data['age'])
plt.title('Age Distribution')
plt.show()
```

Alex: [Analyzing the plot] "We have a few outliers in age. Let's use the IQR method to handle them."

python

Code

```python
# IQR method for outlier detection
Q1 = customer_data['age'].quantile(0.25)
Q3 = customer_data['age'].quantile(0.75)
IQR = Q3 - Q1

# Define outlier bounds
```

```
lower_bound = Q1 - 1.5 * IQR
upper_bound = Q3 + 1.5 * IQR

# Remove outliers
customer_data = customer_data[(customer_data['age'] >= lower_bound) & (customer_data['age'] <= upper_bound)]
```

Alex: [Satisfied] "The customer data is cleaned up. Now, let's move on to the transaction logs."

For the transaction logs, Alex addresses timestamp inconsistencies:

python

Code

```
# Convert timestamps to datetime
transaction_logs['timestamp'] = pd.to_datetime(transaction_logs['timestamp'], errors='coerce')

# Drop rows with invalid timestamps
transaction_logs.dropna(subset=['timestamp'], inplace=True)
```

Alex: [Looking at the market data] "Finally, let's address the outliers in the market data. I'll use Z-score for this."

python

Code

```
from scipy import stats
```

```python
# Convert market data to DataFrame
market_data_df = pd.DataFrame(market_data)

# Calculate Z-scores
z_scores = np.abs(stats.zscore(market_data_df.select_dtypes(include=[np.number])))

# Define a threshold for outliers
threshold = 3

# Identify outliers
outliers = (z_scores > threshold).all(axis=1)

# Remove outliers
market_data_df = market_data_df[~outliers]
```

ADA: [Voice over] "Data cleaning is complete. The customer data is now free of missing values and outliers, the transaction logs have consistent timestamps, and the market data is cleaned of outliers."

---

c. Feature Engineering

Setting: Alex's workstation, now focusing on feature engineering. Alex is brainstorming new features to improve model performance.

Alex: [Thinking aloud] "Feature engineering is crucial for model performance. I need to create new features that could provide additional insights."

ADA: [Voice over] "What features are you planning to engineer today?"

Alex: [Typing] "For customer data, I'll create features such as age groups and purchase frequency. For transaction logs, I'll generate features like total spending per customer. For market data, I'll calculate moving averages and volatility."

Alex starts with the customer data, creating age groups:

python

Code

```
# Define age groups
bins = [0, 18, 30, 40, 50, 60, 100]
labels = ['0-18', '19-30', '31-40', '41-50', '51-60', '60+']
customer_data['age_group'] = pd.cut(customer_data['age'], bins=bins, labels=labels)


# Calculate purchase frequency
customer_data['purchase_frequency'] = customer_data.groupby('customer_id')['purchase_history'].transform('count')
```

Alex: [Nodding] "The new features are added. Now, for the transaction logs, I'll calculate total spending per customer."

python

Code

```
# Calculate total spending per customer
transaction_logs['total_spending'] = transaction_logs.groupby('customer_id')['amount'].transform('sum')
```

Alex: [Satisfied] "That's done. Finally, let's work on the market data."

Alex calculates moving averages and volatility:

python

Code

```
# Convert market data to DataFrame
market_data_df = pd.DataFrame(market_data)

# Calculate moving average and volatility
market_data_df['moving_average'] = market_data_df['price'].rolling(window=7).mean()
market_data_df['volatility'] = market_data_df['price'].rolling(window=7).std()
```

ADA: [Voice over] "Feature engineering is complete. You have new features for customer data, transaction logs, and market data."

Alex: [Leaning back] "Great. The data is now ready for modeling. I'll review these features and integrate them into the model."

Conclusion

During the core work hours, Alex meticulously extracts, preprocesses, and engineers features from the data. Each step, from connecting to data sources and handling missing values to creating new features, plays a crucial role in preparing the data for analysis and modeling.

1. **Data Extraction**: Alex connects to various data sources using SQL, Python scripts, and APIs to gather the required datasets.

2. **Data Cleaning**: Alex employs techniques in Pandas and NumPy to address missing values, outliers, and inconsistencies, ensuring that the data is clean and reliable.

3. **Feature Engineering**: Alex creates new features to enhance model performance, including age groups, purchase frequency, total spending, moving averages, and volatility.

By following these processes, Alex ensures that the data is well-prepared, which is essential for building accurate and effective machine learning models. This thorough approach to data handling exemplifies the meticulous nature of data science and AI research, where attention to detail and systematic processing are key to achieving successful outcomes.

Exploratory Data Analysis (EDA): Unveiling Insights through Visualization and Reporting

Exploratory Data Analysis (EDA) is a crucial phase in the data science workflow. It involves examining datasets to summarize their main characteristics, often employing visual methods to uncover patterns, relationships, and anomalies. EDA is essential for making informed decisions about further analysis and modeling. In this detailed exploration, we'll focus on two main components of EDA: visualization using Matplotlib and Seaborn, and generating insights and reports using PowerBI.

---

1. Visualization: Unveiling Patterns and Relationships

Setting: Alex's workstation, adorned with multiple monitors displaying data visualizations. Alex is preparing to conduct exploratory data analysis.

Alex: [Adjusting monitors] "Alright, let's dive into the data. Visualization is key to understanding our dataset and identifying any patterns or anomalies."

ADA (Alex's Digital Assistant): [Voice over] "Good morning, Alex. You have three datasets ready for visualization: customer data, transaction logs, and market data. Shall I help you with the visualizations?"

Alex: [Nodding] "Yes, please. Let's start with the customer data. I want to explore age distribution, gender distribution, and the relationship between age and purchase frequency."

ADA: [Voice over] "Understood. I'll prepare the data for visualization. You can use Matplotlib and Seaborn for creating the plots."

---

a. Customer Data Visualization

Setting: Alex opens a Jupyter notebook to begin creating visualizations. The data is already loaded into Pandas DataFrames.

Alex: [Typing] "Let's start with the age distribution. I'll use Seaborn to create a histogram."

python

Code

```python
import seaborn as sns
import matplotlib.pyplot as plt

# Load customer data
customer_data = pd.read_sql_query('SELECT * FROM customers', conn)

# Plot age distribution
plt.figure(figsize=(10, 6))
sns.histplot(customer_data['age'], bins=20, kde=True, color='blue')
plt.title('Age Distribution of Customers')
plt.xlabel('Age')
plt.ylabel('Frequency')
```

plt.show()

Alex: [Reviewing the histogram] "This histogram shows that the majority of our customers are between 25 and 45 years old. The KDE curve indicates the overall age distribution."

Alex continues with the gender distribution plot:

python

Code

```
# Plot gender distribution
plt.figure(figsize=(8, 5))
sns.countplot(data=customer_data, x='gender', palette='pastel')
plt.title('Gender Distribution of Customers')
plt.xlabel('Gender')
plt.ylabel('Count')
plt.show()
```

Alex: [Observing the count plot] "The gender distribution is relatively balanced, with a slight skew towards females. Now, let's explore the relationship between age and purchase frequency."

Alex creates a scatter plot with a regression line:

python

Code

```
# Plot age vs. purchase frequency
plt.figure(figsize=(10, 6))
```

```python
sns.regplot(data=customer_data, x='age', y='purchase_frequency', scatter_kws={'color': 'red'}, line_kws={'color': 'green'})
plt.title('Age vs. Purchase Frequency')
plt.xlabel('Age')
plt.ylabel('Purchase Frequency')
plt.show()
```

Alex: [Analyzing the scatter plot] "There seems to be a positive correlation between age and purchase frequency. Older customers tend to have higher purchase frequencies. This insight could be useful for targeted marketing strategies."

---

b. Transaction Logs Visualization

Setting: Alex switches to analyzing transaction logs. The data is loaded and ready.

Alex: [Typing] "Next, let's visualize the transaction logs. I'm interested in examining the total spending per customer and the distribution of transaction amounts."

Alex creates a bar plot for total spending per customer:

python

Code

```python
# Plot total spending per customer
plt.figure(figsize=(12, 6))
top_customers = transaction_logs.groupby('customer_id')['total_spending'].sum().sort_values(ascending=False).head(10)
```

```
sns.barplot(x=top_customers.index, y=top_customers.values, palette='viridis')
plt.title('Top 10 Customers by Total Spending')
plt.xlabel('Customer ID')
plt.ylabel('Total Spending')
plt.xticks(rotation=45)
plt.show()
```

Alex: [Reviewing the bar plot] "These are the top 10 customers by total spending. Identifying high-value customers helps in customizing offers and improving retention strategies."

Alex moves on to analyzing transaction amount distribution:

python

Code

```
# Plot distribution of transaction amounts
plt.figure(figsize=(10, 6))
sns.histplot(transaction_logs['amount'], bins=30, kde=True, color='orange')
plt.title('Distribution of Transaction Amounts')
plt.xlabel('Amount')
plt.ylabel('Frequency')
plt.show()
```

Alex: [Examining the histogram] "The distribution of transaction amounts shows a right skew, with most transactions being relatively small. There are a few large transactions, which could indicate outliers or high-value purchases."

---

c. Market Data Visualization

Setting: Alex now focuses on the market data, which includes price information.

Alex: [Typing] "Finally, let's analyze the market data. I want to see the price trends over time and the volatility."

Alex plots the price trends using a line plot:

python

Code

```
# Convert market data to DataFrame
market_data_df = pd.DataFrame(market_data)


# Plot price trends over time
plt.figure(figsize=(12, 6))
sns.lineplot(data=market_data_df, x='date', y='price', color='purple')
plt.title('Price Trends Over Time')
plt.xlabel('Date')
plt.ylabel('Price')
plt.xticks(rotation=45)
plt.show()
```

Alex: [Observing the line plot] "The price trends show some clear patterns and fluctuations. This could be useful for forecasting and understanding market behavior."

Alex proceeds to visualize volatility:

python

Code

```
# Plot price volatility
plt.figure(figsize=(12, 6))
sns.lineplot(data=market_data_df, x='date', y='volatility', color='teal')
plt.title('Price Volatility Over Time')
plt.xlabel('Date')
plt.ylabel('Volatility')
plt.xticks(rotation=45)
plt.show()
```

Alex: [Analyzing the plot] "The volatility plot indicates periods of high market fluctuation. Understanding this can help in risk assessment and strategic planning."

2. Generating Insights and Reports

Setting: Alex is now preparing to generate a comprehensive report of the EDA findings. The focus is on using PowerBI for creating interactive visualizations and sharing insights.

Alex: [Opening PowerBI] "Next, I need to compile these visualizations into a report. PowerBI will help me create interactive dashboards and share the findings with the team."

ADA: [Voice over] "PowerBI is ready. You can start by importing the datasets and creating visualizations. You can also add interactive elements like filters and slicers to enhance the report."

Alex: [Importing data] "First, I'll import the cleaned datasets into PowerBI. Let's start with the customer data."

Alex imports the customer data into PowerBI and creates a dashboard:

- **Customer Age Distribution**: Using a histogram visual.
- **Gender Distribution**: Using a pie chart.
- **Age vs. Purchase Frequency**: Using a scatter plot with a regression line.

Alex: [Configuring visuals] "I'll add slicers for age groups and gender to allow users to filter and explore the data interactively."

Next, Alex imports the transaction logs:

- **Top Customers by Total Spending**: Using a bar chart.
- **Distribution of Transaction Amounts**: Using a histogram.

Alex: [Adding visuals] "I'll add a slicer for transaction date ranges to enable users to filter transactions based on time periods."

Finally, Alex imports the market data:

- **Price Trends Over Time**: Using a line chart.
- **Price Volatility Over Time**: Using another line chart.

Alex: [Enhancing the report] "I'll include a time slicer to allow users to view price trends and volatility for specific periods."

---

a. Creating Interactive Dashboards

Setting: Alex is refining the interactive elements of the PowerBI report.

Alex: [Configuring interactivity] "I'll set up drill-through actions and tooltips to provide more details when users interact with the visuals."

Alex sets up drill-throughs:

- **For Customer Data:** Users can drill through to see detailed customer profiles.
- **For Transaction Logs:** Users can drill through to view transaction details.

Alex: [Adding tooltips] "Tooltips will display additional information when hovering over data points, enhancing the user experience."

---

b. Sharing and Collaborating

Setting: Alex is ready to share the report with the team.

Alex: [Publishing the report] "The report is ready. I'll publish it to the PowerBI service and share it with the team."

ADA: [Voice over] "Publishing to PowerBI service now. I'll send out notifications to the team members with a link to the report."

Alex shares the report and schedules a meeting to review the findings:

Alex: [Sending invitations] "I've scheduled a meeting for tomorrow to go over the report. This will be a good opportunity to discuss insights and any follow-up actions."

Conclusion

Exploratory Data Analysis (EDA) is a fundamental step in data science, enabling analysts to gain insights and inform subsequent analyses. Here's a summary of the core components of EDA covered in this exploration:

1. **Visualization:**
   - **Customer Data:** Visualization of age distribution, gender distribution, and the relationship between age and purchase frequency using Matplotlib and Seaborn.
   - **Transaction Logs:** Visualization of total spending per customer and distribution of transaction amounts to identify high-value customers and spending patterns.
   - **Market Data:** Visualization of price trends and volatility over time to understand market behavior and fluctuations.

2. **Generating Insights and Reports:**
   - **PowerBI Dashboards:** Importing datasets, creating interactive visualizations, adding slicers and filters, and configuring interactive elements.

- ***Sharing and Collaboration:*** *Publishing the report and scheduling meetings to review findings and discuss next steps.*

Through effective visualization and insightful reporting, Alex transforms raw data into valuable knowledge, driving informed decision-making and strategic planning.

Model Building and Evaluation: A Comprehensive Guide

Model building and evaluation are core components of the data science workflow, transforming clean and preprocessed data into actionable insights through predictive models. This phase involves selecting appropriate algorithms, training models, and evaluating their performance to ensure they meet the desired accuracy and effectiveness. Below, we explore each step in detail, using a dialogue-driven narrative to illustrate the process.

---

1. Select Algorithms: Choosing the Right Tool for the Task

Setting: Alex's workstation, where a new project requires choosing suitable machine learning algorithms. Alex is discussing the approach with ADA, the digital assistant.

Alex: [Reviewing the project brief] "We need to select algorithms for predicting customer churn. The problem involves predicting a categorical outcome—whether a customer will churn or not."

ADA (Alex's Digital Assistant): [Voice over] "For categorical prediction tasks, classification algorithms are most appropriate. Considering the dataset's characteristics and the complexity of the problem, we have several options. Here's a quick overview:"

1. **Logistic Regression:** Simple and interpretable, suitable for binary classification tasks.

2. **Decision Trees:** Useful for capturing non-linear relationships with easy-to-understand visualizations.

3. **Random Forests:** An ensemble method that improves performance by combining multiple decision trees.

4. **Gradient Boosting Machines (GBMs):** Includes algorithms like CatBoost, LightGBM, and XGBoost, known for their high performance in various tasks.

5. **Neural Networks:** Suitable for more complex patterns and larger datasets, implemented using frameworks like TensorFlow and PyTorch.

Alex: [Thinking] "Given the complexity of customer behavior, I'm inclined towards using Gradient Boosting Machines, specifically CatBoost, for its ability to handle categorical features and its robustness. I'll also consider a Random Forest model for comparison."

2. Train Models: Implementing and Training

Setting: Alex's workstation, where the chosen algorithms are to be implemented and trained using Scikit-learn, TensorFlow, and PyTorch.

Alex: [Typing code] "I'll start by implementing and training the models. First, let's set up the environment and prepare the data for training."

Alex loads the preprocessed data:

python

Code

```
import pandas as pd
from sklearn.model_selection import train_test_split

# Load preprocessed data
data = pd.read_csv('preprocessed_customer_data.csv')

# Define features and target variable
X = data.drop('churn', axis=1)
y = data['churn']

# Split data into training and test sets
X_train, X_test, y_train, y_test = train_test_split(X, y, test_size=0.3, random_state=42)
```

ADA: [Voice over] "The data is ready. Let's proceed with training the models."

Alex: [Choosing algorithms] "I'll start with the Random Forest model."

Implementing and training the Random Forest model using Scikit-learn:

python

Code

```python
from sklearn.ensemble import RandomForestClassifier
from sklearn.metrics import classification_report

# Initialize and train the Random Forest model
rf_model = RandomForestClassifier(n_estimators=100, random_state=42)
rf_model.fit(X_train, y_train)

# Make predictions
rf_predictions = rf_model.predict(X_test)

# Evaluate performance
print("Random Forest Model Evaluation:")
print(classification_report(y_test, rf_predictions))
```

Alex: [Reviewing the results] "The Random Forest model is performing well. Now, let's implement and train the CatBoost model."

Implementing and training the CatBoost model:

python

Code

```
from catboost import CatBoostClassifier

# Initialize and train the CatBoost model
catboost_model = CatBoostClassifier(iterations=500, learning_rate=0.1, depth=6, cat_features=[0, 1, 2], verbose=0)
catboost_model.fit(X_train, y_train)

# Make predictions
catboost_predictions = catboost_model.predict(X_test)

# Evaluate performance
print("CatBoost Model Evaluation:")
print(classification_report(y_test, catboost_predictions))
```

Alex: [Nodding] "The CatBoost model also shows strong performance. Lastly, let's explore a neural network using TensorFlow."

Implementing and training a neural network using TensorFlow:

python

Code

```
import tensorflow as tf
from tensorflow.keras.models import Sequential
from tensorflow.keras.layers import Dense
```

```python
# Initialize and build the neural network model
nn_model = Sequential([
    Dense(64, activation='relu', input_shape=(X_train.shape[1],)),
    Dense(32, activation='relu'),
    Dense(1, activation='sigmoid')
])

# Compile the model
nn_model.compile(optimizer='adam', loss='binary_crossentropy', metrics=['accuracy'])

# Train the model
nn_model.fit(X_train, y_train, epochs=10, batch_size=32, validation_split=0.2, verbose=1)

# Evaluate the model
nn_loss, nn_accuracy = nn_model.evaluate(X_test, y_test, verbose=0)
print(f"Neural Network Model Accuracy: {nn_accuracy:.4f}")
```

ADA: [Voice over] "The models have been trained. Now we have results from the Random Forest, CatBoost, and Neural Network models."

Alex: [Reviewing results] "The Random Forest and CatBoost models both have good performance metrics. The neural network accuracy is also promising. Let's summarize the results and decide on the best model."

---

3. Evaluate Performance: Assessing Model Effectiveness

Setting: Alex is now focusing on evaluating and comparing the performance of the trained models.

Alex: [Analyzing performance metrics] "To choose the best model, we need to evaluate performance using various metrics such as accuracy, precision, recall, and F1 score."

ADA: [Voice over] "We have already computed some of these metrics. Let's compare the results from the Random Forest, CatBoost, and Neural Network models."

Alex: [Reviewing classification reports] "The classification reports for the Random Forest and CatBoost models show precision, recall, and F1 score. For the neural network, we have accuracy."

Sample classification report from Scikit-learn:

yaml

Code

Random Forest Model Evaluation:

	precision	recall	f1-score	support
0	0.90	0.85	0.87	1500
1	0.80	0.86	0.83	1300

	precision	recall	f1-score	support
accuracy			0.85	2800
macro avg	0.85	0.85	0.85	2800
weighted avg	0.85	0.85	0.85	2800

Sample classification report from CatBoost:

yaml

Code

CatBoost Model Evaluation:

	precision	recall	f1-score	support
0	0.89	0.87	0.88	1500
1	0.82	0.84	0.83	1300
accuracy			0.86	2800
macro avg	0.86	0.86	0.86	2800
weighted avg	0.86	0.86	0.86	2800

Sample neural network evaluation:

mathematica

Code

Neural Network Model Accuracy: 0.83

Alex: [Summarizing] "The Random Forest and CatBoost models both offer high precision and recall, with CatBoost slightly outperforming Random Forest. The neural network model has a high accuracy but lacks detailed precision and recall metrics in this format."

ADA: [Voice over] "Based on the performance metrics, CatBoost appears to be the best model for this task, offering the best balance between precision and recall."

Alex: [Deciding] "Agreed. CatBoost will be our primary model. We'll use it for final predictions and further analysis. I'll also document the results and methodology for future reference."

Conclusion

The model building and evaluation phase is critical in data science, involving several key steps:

1. **Selecting Algorithms:**
   - **Algorithm Choice:** Based on the problem type, Alex selected CatBoost for its superior handling of categorical features and performance, alongside Random Forest and a Neural Network for comparison.

2. **Training Models:**
   - **Implementation:** Alex implemented and trained the Random Forest, CatBoost, and Neural Network models using Scikit-learn, CatBoost, and TensorFlow.
   - **Training Process:** The models were trained on preprocessed data, and predictions were made on the test set.

3. **Evaluating Performance:**
   - **Metrics:** Performance was evaluated using metrics such as accuracy, precision, recall, and F1 score.

- **Comparison**: The CatBoost model demonstrated the best overall performance, providing a balanced trade-off between precision and recall.

By following this comprehensive approach, Alex ensures that the selected model is well-suited for the task, effectively predicting customer churn and driving actionable business insights. The detailed evaluation helps in making informed decisions and optimizing model performance for real-world applications.

Model Deployment: From

Development to Production

Deploying machine learning models is a crucial step in transitioning from model development to practical application. This phase involves setting up the model for real-world use, integrating it into applications, and ensuring its performance and reliability. We will delve into the deployment process, including setting up APIs with Flask or FastAPI and containerizing the application using Docker. We'll also explore monitoring strategies to ensure the model's ongoing effectiveness.

1. Model Deployment: Moving from Local to Production

Setting: Alex is preparing to deploy the CatBoost model, which has been selected as the best model for predicting customer churn. The goal is to make the model available through an API that can be integrated into a web application.

Alex: [Reviewing deployment steps] "Now that we have the model trained and evaluated, it's time to deploy it. We'll start by setting up an API to allow the model to interact with other applications."

ADA (Alex's Digital Assistant): [Voice over] "For deployment, we'll use Flask or FastAPI to create a RESTful API. Then, we'll containerize the application using Docker to ensure consistency and scalability."

Alex: [Choosing Flask] "I'll use Flask for the API. It's simple and widely used. Let's get started."

ADA: [Voice over] "Great choice. I'll help you set up the Flask application."

Setting up Flask API for model deployment:

1. **Create the Flask Application**

Setting: Alex creates a new Python file for the Flask application.

python

Code

```
from flask import Flask, request, jsonify
import catboost
import pandas as pd

# Load the trained model
model = catboost.CatBoostClassifier()
model.load_model('catboost_model.cbm')

app = Flask(__name__)

@app.route('/predict', methods=['POST'])
def predict():
    try:
        # Get the data from the request
        data = request.json
```

```python
        df = pd.DataFrame(data)

        # Make predictions
        predictions = model.predict(df)

        # Send the predictions back as JSON
        return jsonify(predictions.tolist())
    except Exception as e:
        return jsonify({'error': str(e)})

if __name__ == '__main__':
    app.run(host='0.0.0.0', port=5000, debug=True)
```

Alex: [Reviewing the code] "This Flask application exposes an endpoint /predict that accepts POST requests with JSON data, makes predictions using the CatBoost model, and returns the results."

2. **Test the Flask API Locally**

Setting: Alex runs the Flask application to test it locally.

bash

Code

```
python app.py
```

ADA: [Voice over] "The Flask server is running. You can now test the API using tools like Postman or cURL."

Testing with cURL:

bash

Code

curl -X POST http://localhost:5000/predict -H "Content-Type: application/json" -d '[{"feature1": value1, "feature2": value2, ...}]'

Alex: [Reviewing the results] "The API is working correctly and returning predictions as expected. Now, let's move on to containerizing the application with Docker."

---

2. Containerizing the Application with Docker

Setting: Alex is preparing to containerize the Flask application to ensure it runs consistently across different environments.

Alex: [Reviewing Docker setup] "Containerizing the application will help in managing dependencies and ensuring that the environment is consistent across different machines."

ADA: [Voice over] "We'll use Docker to create an image of the Flask application. This involves writing a Dockerfile and building the Docker image."

1. Create a Dockerfile

Setting: Alex creates a Dockerfile in the project directory.

dockerfile

Code

```
# Use the official Python image from the Docker Hub
FROM python:3.9-slim
```

```
# Set the working directory
WORKDIR /app

# Copy the requirements file and install dependencies
COPY requirements.txt requirements.txt
RUN pip install -r requirements.txt

# Copy the Flask application code
COPY . .

# Expose port 5000
EXPOSE 5000

# Define the command to run the Flask application
CMD ["python", "app.py"]
```

2. **Create a Requirements File**

Setting: Alex creates a requirements.txt file listing the dependencies.

text

Code

```
flask
catboost
pandas
```

3. **Build and Run the Docker Container**

Setting: Alex uses Docker commands to build and run the container.

bash

Code

Build the Docker image

docker build -t flask-catboost-app .

Run the Docker container

docker run -p 5000:5000 flask-catboost-app

ADA: [Voice over] "The Docker container is up and running. You can now access the Flask API on port 5000 of your host machine."

Alex: [Testing in Docker] "The container is working as expected. The API is accessible and returning predictions."

---

3. Monitoring: Ensuring Continuous Performance

Setting: Alex is setting up monitoring to ensure that the deployed model continues to perform well and responds accurately to requests.

Alex: [Reviewing monitoring strategies] "Monitoring is crucial to ensure that the model performs well in production and any issues are addressed promptly."

ADA: [Voice over] "For monitoring, consider the following strategies:

1. **Performance Monitoring**: Track API response times and error rates.

2. **Model Performance**: Monitor model predictions and assess performance over time.
3. **Logging**: Capture logs for debugging and auditing purposes."
4. **Set Up Performance Monitoring**

Setting: Alex integrates performance monitoring using a tool like Prometheus or an application performance monitoring (APM) service.

Alex: [Integrating with Prometheus] "I'll set up Prometheus to track API metrics. This involves instrumenting the Flask application with a monitoring library."

Integrating Flask with Prometheus:

python

Code

```python
from prometheus_flask_exporter import PrometheusMetrics

# Initialize Prometheus metrics
metrics = PrometheusMetrics(app)

# Track request duration
metrics.info('flask_app', 'Flask Application')
```

ADA: [Voice over] "With Prometheus integrated, you can track metrics like request duration, error rates, and request counts."

2. **Monitor Model Performance**

Setting: Alex implements logging to monitor model predictions and evaluate performance over time.

Alex: *[Setting up logging]* *"I'll log prediction results and compare them against actual outcomes to monitor model drift and performance."*

Logging predictions and actual outcomes:

python

Code

```python
import logging

# Configure logging
logging.basicConfig(filename='model_predictions.log', level=logging.INFO)

@app.route('/predict', methods=['POST'])
def predict():
    try:
        data = request.json
        df = pd.DataFrame(data)
        predictions = model.predict(df)

        # Log predictions
        logging.info(f"Predictions: {predictions.tolist()}")

        return jsonify(predictions.tolist())
```

```
except Exception as e:
    logging.error(f"Error: {str(e)}")
    return jsonify({'error': str(e)})
```

ADA: [Voice over] "By logging predictions and errors, you can review historical data and identify any trends or issues."

3. Set Up Alerts

Setting: Alex sets up alerts to notify the team of any anomalies or performance issues.

Alex: [Configuring alerts] "I'll use a monitoring tool that supports alerts to notify us if the API response time exceeds a threshold or if there are unexpected errors."

ADA: [Voice over] "Alerts will help you quickly address any issues that arise, minimizing downtime and ensuring continuous performance."

Conclusion

The deployment phase is essential for transitioning machine learning models from development to real-world applications. Here's a summary of the core components of the deployment process:

1. **Model Deployment:**
   - **API Setup:** Created a Flask API to expose the CatBoost model, allowing it to interact with other applications.
   - **Containerization:** Used Docker to containerize the Flask application, ensuring consistent deployment across different environments.

2. **Monitoring:**
    - **Performance Monitoring:** Integrated Prometheus for tracking API metrics such as response times and error rates.
    - **Model Performance:** Implemented logging to monitor predictions and assess model performance over time.
    - **Alerts:** Configured alerts to notify the team of any performance issues or anomalies.

By following these steps, Alex ensures that the model is deployed effectively and monitored continuously, providing reliable and accurate predictions in a production environment. This comprehensive approach helps in maintaining model performance and addressing any issues promptly, ensuring the model delivers value and meets business objectives.

Afternoon Routine: Feedback and Retraining in Model Deployment

In the afternoon routine of a data scientist or AI researcher, the focus shifts towards maintaining and improving model performance through feedback and retraining. This stage is crucial for adapting to changes in data and user needs, ensuring that the deployed model remains accurate and effective. Let's explore this routine in depth through a detailed, dialogue-driven narrative.

1. Collect Feedback: Gathering Performance Data and User Insights

Setting: Alex's office, where the focus is now on collecting feedback and performance data from the deployed CatBoost model. Alex is discussing the plan with ADA, the digital assistant.

Alex: [Reviewing data] "We need to assess how the CatBoost model is performing in production. To do this, we'll gather feedback from users and collect performance data from the system."

ADA (Alex's Digital Assistant): [Voice over] "Collecting feedback is essential for understanding user experiences and model performance. Here's how we can approach this:"

1. User Feedback Collection

Setting: Alex is setting up a mechanism to collect feedback from users interacting with the model.

Alex: [Configuring feedback collection] "We'll integrate a feedback form into the application interface. Users can provide their input on the model's predictions."

Creating a feedback form:

html

Code

```html
<form action="/feedback" method="POST">
    <label for="prediction">Prediction:</label>
    <input type="text" id="prediction" name="prediction" required>
```

```html
<label for="actual">Actual Outcome:</label>
<input type="text" id="actual" name="actual" required>

<label for="comments">Additional Comments:</label>
<textarea id="comments" name="comments"></textarea>

<button type="submit">Submit Feedback</button>
</form>
```

ADA: [Voice over] "The feedback form will collect the prediction, actual outcome, and any additional comments from users."

2. Performance Data Collection

Setting: Alex is configuring the system to log performance metrics and prediction outcomes.

Alex: [Setting up logging] "We'll log the model's predictions along with the actual outcomes. This will help us analyze how well the model is performing over time."

Implementing logging in the Flask application:

python

Code

```
import logging

# Configure logging
```

```
logging.basicConfig(filename='model_feedback.log', level=logging.INFO)


@app.route('/feedback', methods=['POST'])
def feedback():
    try:
        data = request.form
        prediction = data.get('prediction')
        actual = data.get('actual')
        comments = data.get('comments')

        # Log feedback
        logging.info(f"Prediction: {prediction}, Actual: {actual}, Comments: {comments}")

        return "Feedback submitted successfully"
    except Exception as e:
        logging.error(f"Error: {str(e)}")
        return "Error submitting feedback"
```

ADA: [Voice over] "With the feedback and performance data collected, we'll have a comprehensive view of the model's effectiveness and areas for improvement."

Alex: [Reviewing data] "We've set up the feedback collection and performance logging. Next, we'll review the collected data to identify patterns and areas for improvement."

2. Retrain Models: Updating and Improving

Setting: Alex is analyzing the feedback and performance data collected over the past few weeks. The focus is now on retraining the model to improve its accuracy and address any issues identified.

Alex: [Reviewing feedback and performance logs] "The feedback indicates some discrepancies between predictions and actual outcomes. We need to retrain the model using the new data to enhance its performance."

ADA: [Voice over] "Retraining involves several steps:

1. **Data Preparation:** Aggregate the feedback and performance data to create a new dataset for retraining.

2. **Model Training:** Use the new dataset to retrain the model, incorporating feedback to improve accuracy.

3. **Evaluation:** Assess the retrained model's performance to ensure improvements."

4. **Data Preparation**

Setting: Alex is aggregating feedback and performance data to prepare a new dataset.

Alex: [Aggregating data] "We'll start by cleaning and preparing the data from feedback logs and performance metrics."

Data preparation process:

python

Code

```python
import pandas as pd

# Load feedback data
feedback_data = pd.read_csv('model_feedback.log', delimiter=' ', header=None, names=['timestamp', 'prediction', 'actual', 'comments'])

# Clean and preprocess data
feedback_data['prediction'] = feedback_data['prediction'].astype(float)
feedback_data['actual'] = feedback_data['actual'].astype(float)

# Prepare dataset for retraining
X_retrain = feedback_data[['prediction']]
y_retrain = feedback_data['actual']
```

ADA: [Voice over] "With the data prepared, we can now proceed with retraining the model."

2. Model Training

Setting: Alex is using the new dataset to retrain the CatBoost model.

Alex: [Retraining the model] "We'll use the feedback data to retrain the CatBoost model, incorporating the new information to improve its accuracy."

Retraining the model using CatBoost:

python

Code

```
from catboost import CatBoostClassifier

# Initialize the retrained CatBoost model
retrained_model = CatBoostClassifier(iterations=500, learning_rate=0.1, depth=6, cat_features=[0, 1, 2])

# Train the model with the new dataset
retrained_model.fit(X_retrain, y_retrain)

# Save the retrained model
retrained_model.save_model('catboost_retrained_model.cbm')
```

ADA: [Voice over] "The model has been retrained with the updated data. The next step is to evaluate its performance."

3. Model Evaluation

Setting: Alex is evaluating the performance of the retrained model to ensure that it has improved.

Alex: [Evaluating the retrained model] "We'll assess the performance of the retrained model using a validation set to ensure it shows improvements."

Evaluating the retrained model:

python

Code

```
from sklearn.metrics import classification_report
```

```python
# Load the validation data
validation_data = pd.read_csv('validation_data.csv')

# Prepare validation data
X_val = validation_data[['feature1', 'feature2', ...]]
y_val = validation_data['target']

# Make predictions with the retrained model
val_predictions = retrained_model.predict(X_val)

# Evaluate performance
print("Retrained CatBoost Model Evaluation:")
print(classification_report(y_val, val_predictions))
```

ADA: [Voice over] "The evaluation will help confirm whether the retrained model performs better and meets the desired accuracy."

Alex: [Reviewing evaluation results] "The retrained model shows significant improvements in accuracy and reduced discrepancies between predictions and actual outcomes. We're ready to deploy the updated model."

Conclusion

The afternoon routine of feedback and retraining is critical for maintaining and improving model performance in production. Here's a summary of the key steps involved:

1. **Collect Feedback:**
    - **User Feedback:** Integrated a feedback form to gather user input on predictions and outcomes.
    - **Performance Data:** Configured logging to capture model predictions and actual outcomes, providing a comprehensive view of performance.

2. **Retrain Models:**
    - **Data Preparation:** Aggregated and cleaned feedback and performance data to create a new dataset for retraining.
    - **Model Training:** Retrained the CatBoost model using the new dataset, incorporating feedback to enhance accuracy.
    - **Model Evaluation:** Evaluated the retrained model to ensure improvements in performance.

By following these steps, Alex ensures that the deployed model remains effective and accurate, continually adapting to new data and user feedback. This iterative process helps in optimizing model performance and ensuring that the model delivers valuable insights and accurate predictions.

Tech Stack Overview: CRUD Operations

CRUD operations form the backbone of data management in modern software systems. Understanding and implementing these operations effectively is essential for managing data and models across various tech stacks, from relational databases to cloud-based data services. This comprehensive guide provides a detailed overview of CRUD operations, including their definitions, practical implementations, and best practices.

1. Overview of CRUD Operations

CRUD stands for Create, Read, Update, and Delete. These operations are fundamental for interacting with and manipulating data within a system. Each operation corresponds to a basic function required to manage and maintain data in a persistent storage system.

1.1. Create

Create involves adding new data to a system. This operation is crucial for initializing records or inserting new entries into a database or data model.

Implementation Strategies:

- **SQL Databases**: Use the INSERT statement to add new records. For example:

sql

Code

INSERT INTO users (username, email, password) VALUES ('john_doe', 'john@example.com', 'securepassword');

- **NoSQL Databases**: In databases like MongoDB, use methods like insertOne or insertMany:

javascript

Code

db.users.insertOne({ username: 'john_doe', email: 'john@example.com', password: 'securepassword' });

- **APIs**: For RESTful APIs, a POST request to a specific endpoint (e.g., /users) with the data payload is used:

http

Code

POST /users

Content-Type: application/json

```
{
  "username": "john_doe",
  "email": "john@example.com",
  "password": "securepassword"
}
```

Best Practices:

- **Validation**: Ensure that data is validated before creating a record to maintain data integrity.
- **Transactions**: Use transactions to ensure that the creation of data is atomic, especially when multiple related records are being inserted.
- **Error Handling**: Implement proper error handling to manage issues that may arise during the creation process, such as duplicate entries or constraint violations.

1.2. Read

Read involves retrieving data from a system. This operation is essential for querying and displaying data based on various criteria.

Implementation Strategies:

- **SQL Databases**: Use the SELECT statement to query data. For example:

sql

Code

```sql
SELECT * FROM users WHERE username = 'john_doe';
```

- **NoSQL Databases**: Use methods like find or findOne to retrieve data:

javascript

Code

db.users.findOne({ username: 'john_doe' });

- **APIs**: For RESTful APIs, a GET request to a specific endpoint (e.g., /users/{id}) retrieves the data:

http

Code

GET /users/john_doe

Best Practices:

- **Indexing**: Use indexing to improve query performance, especially for large datasets.
- **Pagination**: Implement pagination to handle large volumes of data and improve response times.
- **Caching**: Use caching mechanisms to reduce the load on the database and speed up data retrieval.

1.3. Update

Update involves modifying existing data in a system. This operation is crucial for reflecting changes and keeping data current.

Implementation Strategies:

- **SQL Databases**: Use the UPDATE statement to modify records. For example:

sql

Code

UPDATE users SET email = 'new_email@example.com' WHERE username = 'john_doe';

- **NoSQL Databases**: Use methods like updateOne or updateMany:

javascript

Code

db.users.updateOne({ username: 'john_doe' }, { $set: { email: 'new_email@example.com' } });

- **APIs**: For RESTful APIs, a PUT or PATCH request to a specific endpoint (e.g., /users/{id}) with the updated data payload is used:

http

Code

PUT /users/john_doe

Content-Type: application/json

{
  "email": "new_email@example.com"
}

Best Practices:

- **Concurrency Control**: Implement mechanisms to handle concurrent updates and prevent data conflicts, such as optimistic or pessimistic locking.
- **Partial Updates**: Use partial updates (PATCH) for scenarios where only specific fields need to be modified.
- **Auditing**: Maintain an audit trail of changes to track modifications and revert if necessary.

1.4. Delete

Delete involves removing data from a system. This operation is essential for managing data lifecycle and ensuring data accuracy.

Implementation Strategies:

- **SQL Databases:** Use the DELETE statement to remove records. For example:

sql

Code

```
DELETE FROM users WHERE username = 'john_doe';
```

- **NoSQL Databases:** Use methods like deleteOne or deleteMany:

javascript

Code

```
db.users.deleteOne({ username: 'john_doe' });
```

- **APIs:** For RESTful APIs, a DELETE request to a specific endpoint (e.g., /users/{id}) removes the data:

http

Code

```
DELETE /users/john_doe
```

Best Practices:

- **Soft Deletes:** Implement soft deletes where records are marked as deleted but not physically removed, allowing for data recovery if needed.
- **Cascade Deletion:** Use cascade deletion to ensure related records are also deleted, but be cautious as it can lead to unintended data loss.

- **Data Integrity**: Ensure that deletion operations do not violate data integrity constraints or lead to orphaned records.

2. CRUD Operations in Various Tech Stacks

2.1. Relational Databases

Relational databases (e.g., MySQL, PostgreSQL) use SQL for managing data. CRUD operations are implemented through SQL statements and transactions.

- **Create**: INSERT statements are used to add new rows to tables.
- **Read**: SELECT statements are used to query data from tables.
- **Update**: UPDATE statements are used to modify existing rows.
- **Delete**: DELETE statements are used to remove rows from tables.

2.2. NoSQL Databases

NoSQL databases (e.g., MongoDB, Cassandra) use various methods for CRUD operations. They are designed to handle unstructured data and provide scalability.

- **Create**: Methods like insertOne or insertMany add documents to collections.
- **Read**: Methods like find or findOne retrieve documents based on query criteria.
- **Update**: Methods like updateOne or updateMany modify existing documents.
- **Delete**: Methods like deleteOne or deleteMany remove documents from collections.

2.3. Cloud-Based Data Services

Cloud-based data services (e.g., AWS DynamoDB, Google Cloud Firestore) provide managed data storage solutions with built-in scalability and reliability.

- **Create**: Use service-specific APIs to add new data.
- **Read**: Use query and scan methods to retrieve data.
- **Update**: Use update methods to modify existing data.
- **Delete**: Use delete methods to remove data from the service.

2.4. APIs and Web Services

APIs and web services provide a way to interact with data and models over the web. CRUD operations are implemented through HTTP methods in RESTful APIs or other protocols in different API architectures.

- **Create**: POST requests are used to create new resources.
- **Read**: GET requests are used to retrieve resources.
- **Update**: PUT or PATCH requests are used to update existing resources.
- **Delete**: DELETE requests are used to remove resources.

3. Best Practices for CRUD Operations

3.1. Security

- **Authentication and Authorization**: Implement authentication to verify user identities and authorization to ensure users have the right permissions to perform CRUD operations.

- **Data Encryption**: Encrypt sensitive data to protect it from unauthorized access.

3.2. Performance Optimization

- **Indexing**: Create indexes on columns frequently used in queries to improve read performance.
- **Query Optimization**: Optimize queries to reduce execution time and resource usage.

3.3. Data Integrity

- **Validation**: Validate input data to prevent incorrect or malicious data from being stored.
- **Constraints**: Use database constraints to enforce data integrity rules.

3.4. Scalability

- **Horizontal Scaling**: Implement horizontal scaling strategies to handle increased data volume and traffic.
- **Load Balancing**: Use load balancers to distribute incoming requests across multiple servers.

3.5. Backup and Recovery

- **Regular Backups**: Perform regular backups to protect data from loss or corruption.
- **Disaster Recovery**: Implement disaster recovery plans to ensure data can be restored in case of a failure.

3.6. Documentation

- **API Documentation**: Provide clear documentation for APIs, including information on endpoints, request formats, and response structures.

- ***Database Schema***: Document the database schema, including table structures, relationships, and constraints.

Conclusion

CRUD operations—Create, Read, Update, Delete—are fundamental to managing data and models across various tech stacks. Understanding and implementing these operations effectively is crucial for maintaining data integrity, performance, and scalability. By following best practices and leveraging appropriate technologies, developers and data professionals can ensure that CRUD operations are handled efficiently and securely.

This comprehensive guide covers the essential aspects of CRUD operations, their implementation in different contexts, and best practices for optimal data management. Mastery of CRUD operations is key to building robust, reliable, and scalable data-driven applications.

This extensive guide provides a thorough understanding of CRUD operations, tailored for different tech stacks and best practices. Implementing these practices will help in effectively managing data and models in various environments.

Collaboration and Communication in Data Science and Software Development

Effective collaboration and communication are crucial in any team-based environment, especially in fields like data science and software development where complex projects require diverse expertise and seamless integration of work. This guide covers best practices for team discussions and documentation to ensure productivity and project success.

Team Discussions

Importance of Team Discussions

Team discussions are central to successful project development. They facilitate the exchange of ideas, alignment of goals, and collective problem-solving.

Regular and effective discussions can significantly impact the progress and quality of the work by leveraging the collective expertise of team members.

Types of Discussions

1. **Brainstorming Sessions**: These are informal meetings aimed at generating ideas and exploring creative solutions. During brainstorming, all ideas are welcomed without immediate critique. This encourages open communication and innovation.

2. **Code Reviews**: A structured review of code to identify bugs, optimize performance, and ensure adherence to coding standards. Code reviews improve code quality and foster knowledge sharing among team members.

3. **Project Updates**: Regular updates on progress, roadblocks, and changes in project scope. These discussions keep everyone on the same page and help in adjusting plans as needed.

4. **Problem-Solving Meetings**: Focused discussions on specific challenges or issues faced in the project. These meetings aim to find effective solutions through collaborative effort.

Best Practices for Effective Team Discussions

1. **Set Clear Objectives**: Ensure that every discussion has a clear goal. This helps in staying focused and productive. For example, a brainstorming session might aim to generate new feature ideas, while a code review should focus on code quality.

2. **Encourage Participation**: Create an environment where everyone feels comfortable sharing their ideas

and opinions. This inclusivity leads to a richer discussion and more innovative solutions.

3. **Stay Organized**: Use structured formats for discussions, such as agendas for meetings and checklists for code reviews. This helps in keeping track of topics covered and actions needed.

4. **Document Outcomes**: Summarize key points, decisions made, and action items at the end of each discussion. This ensures that everyone is aware of what was agreed upon and what needs to be done next.

5. **Foster Respectful Communication**: Encourage respectful dialogue, even when disagreements arise. Constructive feedback should be given with the intent to improve and support each other.

6. **Leverage Technology**: Utilize tools like video conferencing, collaborative document editing, and project management software to facilitate discussions, especially in remote teams.

Documentation

Importance of Documentation

Documentation is essential for tracking the progress and details of a project. It serves as a reference for current and future team members, ensures consistency, and facilitates easier maintenance and scaling of the project.

Types of Documentation

1. **Model Configurations**: Document the parameters, algorithms, and settings used in machine learning models. This helps in replicating results,

troubleshooting issues, and comparing different models.

2. **Data Preprocessing Steps**: Detail the methods used to clean, transform, and prepare data for analysis or model training. This includes data cleaning techniques, feature engineering, and normalization methods.

3. **Deployment Details**: Record the procedures and configurations for deploying the model or software, including environment setup, dependencies, and deployment scripts.

4. **Code Documentation**: Provide comments and explanations within the code to make it understandable for others. This includes describing the purpose of functions, variables, and complex logic.

5. **Project Documentation**: Maintain comprehensive documentation of the project's objectives, requirements, design decisions, and progress. This includes project plans, timelines, and milestone reviews.

Best Practices for Effective Documentation

1. **Be Clear and Concise**: Write documentation in a way that is easy to understand. Avoid jargon and overly technical language unless necessary, and provide explanations where needed.

2. **Update Regularly**: Keep documentation current with the latest changes in the project. Outdated documentation can lead to confusion and errors.

3. **Use Templates**: Implement standardized templates for different types of documentation to ensure consistency and completeness. This makes it easier to create and review documentation.

4. **Incorporate Visuals**: Use diagrams, charts, and screenshots to complement written explanations. Visuals can make complex information more digestible and understandable.

5. **Review and Revise**: Regularly review documentation for accuracy and relevance. Solicit feedback from team members to identify areas for improvement and ensure that the documentation meets the needs of its users.

6. **Make Documentation Accessible**: Store documentation in a centralized location that is easily accessible to all team members. Use version control systems to manage changes and maintain history.

Integration of Collaboration and Documentation

Seamless Integration

The interplay between collaboration and documentation is vital for project success. Effective communication should be reflected in thorough and up-to-date documentation, and vice versa. Here's how to integrate these aspects seamlessly:

1. **Align Documentation with Discussions**: Ensure that the outcomes of team discussions are accurately reflected in the documentation. For instance, if a new approach is decided during a meeting, update the relevant documents accordingly.

2. ***Use Documentation to Facilitate Discussions***: Well-maintained documentation can serve as a reference point during discussions, helping to clarify points, provide context, and support decision-making.

3. ***Implement Collaborative Documentation Tools***: Utilize tools that allow multiple team members to contribute to and review documentation in real-time. This enhances collaboration and ensures that documentation is always up-to-date.

4. ***Track Changes and Decisions***: Document changes in project direction or decisions made during discussions. This creates a historical record that can be reviewed later if needed.

5. ***Create a Feedback Loop***: Encourage team members to provide feedback on documentation and discussions. This continuous loop of input and revision helps in improving both collaboration and documentation quality.

Conclusion

Effective collaboration and communication are cornerstones of successful project development in data science and software engineering. By actively engaging in team discussions and maintaining thorough documentation, teams can ensure that projects are executed efficiently and meet their objectives. Emphasizing clear objectives, inclusive participation, and regular updates in discussions, along with clear, concise, and accessible documentation, will foster a productive and collaborative environment, ultimately leading to more successful outcomes.

This guide provides a framework for understanding and implementing effective collaboration and communication strategies. Tailoring these practices to fit the specific needs and dynamics of your team will further enhance their effectiveness.

End-of-Day Procedures for Data Science and Software

Development Professionals

Managing end-of-day activities effectively is crucial for maintaining productivity, ensuring smooth project progress, and supporting continuous professional growth. This guide delves into two primary areas: wrapping up daily work and dedicating time to learning and development.

1. Wrap-Up

Importance of Wrapping Up

Wrapping up at the end of the day ensures that you leave with a clear understanding of what has been accomplished and what needs to be done next. It provides closure for the day's tasks, allows you to set clear priorities for the next day, and helps in maintaining a well-organized workflow. This process also helps in managing time effectively, reducing stress, and improving overall productivity.

Steps to Review Progress

1. **Review Completed Tasks:**
   - **Check Task Lists:** Go through your task lists or project management tools (e.g., Jira, Trello, Asana) to review which tasks have been completed. Mark off tasks that are finished and update their status.

- **Verify Deliverables**: Ensure that all deliverables (e.g., code commits, model outputs, documentation) meet the required quality standards. Double-check for any issues or incomplete elements.

2. **Update Project Statuses**:
    - **Project Tracking Tools**: Update project tracking tools with the latest status. This might include adjusting timelines, updating progress bars, or revising task statuses.
    - **Team Communication**: Communicate updates to relevant team members. This can be done through team channels (e.g., Slack, Microsoft Teams) or project management tools. Ensure that everyone is aware of the current status and any changes.

3. **Document Achievements and Challenges**:
    - **Daily Log**: Maintain a daily log or journal where you document what was achieved, any challenges encountered, and how they were addressed. This helps in reflecting on daily progress and identifying patterns or recurring issues.
    - **Notes for Next Steps**: Make notes about any unfinished tasks or new issues that need to be addressed. This ensures a smooth transition to the next workday.

4. **Assess Time Management**:
    - **Evaluate Time Spent**: Review how much time was spent on various tasks. Assess whether this

aligns with your planned schedule and identify any areas where time management can be improved.

- **Adjust Priorities:** Based on your assessment, adjust priorities for the next day. If certain tasks took longer than expected, consider revising your approach or allocating more time.

Planning for Tomorrow

1. **Set Goals for the Next Day:**

    - **Define Objectives:** Set clear and achievable goals for the next day. These should be specific, measurable, and aligned with the overall project objectives.
    - **Prioritize Tasks:** Prioritize tasks based on their importance and urgency. Ensure that critical tasks are given precedence to avoid bottlenecks.

2. **Create a Task List:**

    - **Daily To-Do List:** Create a to-do list for the next day that includes all the tasks you plan to accomplish. Break down larger tasks into smaller, manageable steps.
    - **Time Estimates:** Estimate the time required for each task. This helps in creating a realistic schedule and ensures that you allocate sufficient time for each activity.

3. **Prepare for Meetings and Collaborations:**

    - **Review Meeting Agendas:** Check if there are any meetings scheduled for the next day and review their agendas. Prepare any materials or reports needed for these meetings.

- **Coordinate with Team Members**: If you need to collaborate with others, make sure to communicate any necessary information or updates in advance.

4. *Plan for Interruptions:*

- **Identify Potential Interruptions**: Anticipate any potential interruptions or challenges that might arise and plan how to address them.
- **Buffer Time**: Allocate buffer time in your schedule to handle unexpected issues or delays.

5. *Reflect and Adjust:*

- **Reflect on the Day**: Take a few moments to reflect on what went well and what could be improved. Use this reflection to make adjustments to your workflow or approach for the next day.
- **Adjust Plans**: Based on your reflection, adjust your plans and goals as needed. Flexibility is key to adapting to changing circumstances.

2. Learning and Development

Importance of Learning and Development

Continuous learning and development are essential for staying current with industry trends, mastering new technologies, and enhancing professional skills. In fields like data science and software development, where technology evolves rapidly, ongoing education helps maintain a competitive edge and supports career growth.

Allocating Time for Learning

1. **Schedule Learning Time:**
   - **Dedicated Learning Sessions:** Allocate specific time slots during your week dedicated solely to learning. This could be daily, weekly, or bi-weekly, depending on your schedule and learning goals.
   - **Balance with Work:** Ensure that your learning time is balanced with work responsibilities. Avoid overloading yourself with too many simultaneous tasks.

2. **Set Learning Goals:**
   - **Define Objectives:** Set clear learning objectives. This could include mastering a new tool, understanding a new concept, or achieving a certification.
   - **Create a Learning Plan:** Develop a structured learning plan with milestones and deadlines. This helps in staying focused and tracking progress.

Exploring New Technologies

1. **New Tools and Frameworks:**
   - **Streamlit:** Explore tools like Streamlit for creating interactive dashboards. Streamlit allows for rapid development of web applications for data science projects with

minimal code. Familiarize yourself with its features, such as widgets and layout options.

- **Other Technologies**: Stay informed about other emerging technologies and tools relevant to your field. This might include new libraries in Python, advanced machine learning frameworks, or innovative software development practices.

2. **Advanced Concepts in Deep Learning**:

- **Deep Learning Algorithms**: Study advanced deep learning algorithms, such as Generative Adversarial Networks (GANs), Reinforcement Learning, or Transfer Learning. Understanding these concepts can enhance your ability to tackle complex problems.

- **Hands-On Projects**: Apply your knowledge through hands-on projects. Implement deep learning models, experiment with different architectures, and evaluate their performance on real-world datasets.

Continuous Skill Improvement

1. **Online Courses and Tutorials**:

- **Enroll in Courses**: Take advantage of online courses and tutorials offered by platforms like Coursera, edX, Udacity, or Khan Academy. These platforms offer a wide range of courses on data science, machine learning, and software development.

- **Certifications**: Consider pursuing certifications that validate your skills and knowledge.

Certifications can be beneficial for career advancement and demonstrate your expertise to potential employers.

2. **Reading and Research:**
   - **Research Papers:** *Read research papers and articles related to your field. This helps in staying updated with the latest developments and understanding cutting-edge techniques.*
   - **Books and Blogs:** *Follow industry blogs and read books written by experts in data science and software development. These resources provide valuable insights and practical knowledge.*

3. **Networking and Community Involvement:**
   - **Join Professional Communities:** *Engage with professional communities and forums related to your field. Participate in discussions, ask questions, and share your knowledge with others.*
   - **Attend Conferences and Meetups:** *Attend industry conferences, webinars, and meetups to network with peers, learn about new trends, and gain insights from experts.*

4. **Practice and Experimentation:**
   - **Build Projects:** *Work on personal or open-source projects to apply new skills and technologies. Building projects helps in reinforcing learning and gaining practical experience.*
   - **Experiment with New Techniques:** *Experiment with new techniques and approaches in your*

projects. This hands-on practice enhances your problem-solving skills and adaptability.

Evaluating and Reflecting on Learning

1. **Assess Progress:**
   - **Track Achievements:** Regularly assess your progress towards learning goals. Review what you have accomplished and identify areas where further improvement is needed.
   - **Update Learning Plan:** Based on your progress assessment, update your learning plan and set new goals as needed.

2. **Reflect on Learning Outcomes:**
   - **Apply Knowledge:** Reflect on how newly acquired skills and knowledge have been applied in your work. Consider the impact on project outcomes and personal growth.
   - **Seek Feedback:** Seek feedback from peers or mentors on your learning progress. Constructive feedback helps in identifying strengths and areas for improvement.

Conclusion

End-of-day wrap-up procedures and continuous learning are integral to achieving success and growth in data science and software development. By reviewing progress, planning effectively for the next day, and dedicating time to learning and development, professionals can ensure that they remain productive, proficient, and competitive in their fields. This structured approach not only enhances daily performance but also supports long-term career advancement and personal fulfillment.

This comprehensive guide provides a detailed framework for managing end-of-day activities and pursuing ongoing professional development. Implementing these practices will help in maintaining a productive workflow and staying at the forefront of industry advancements.

Machine Learning Algorithms: Linear Regression, CatBoost, Neural Networks

Machine learning (ML) algorithms are the foundation of predictive modeling and data analysis. This guide provides an in-depth exploration of three important ML algorithms: Linear Regression, CatBoost, and Neural Networks. Each algorithm serves different purposes and excels in various tasks, from basic regression problems to complex classification and prediction tasks.

1. Linear Regression

1.1. Overview

Linear Regression is one of the simplest and most commonly used algorithms in machine learning and statistics. It is used to model the relationship between a dependent variable and one or more independent variables by fitting a linear equation to observed data.

1.2. Mathematical Foundation

The goal of Linear Regression is to find the best-fitting line through the data points. This line is defined by the equation:

y=β0+β1x1+β2x2+⋯+βnxn+□y = \beta_0 + \beta_1 x_1 + \beta_2 x_2 + \cdots + \beta_n x_n + \epsilony=β0+β1x1+β2x2+⋯+βnxn+□

where:

- yyy is the dependent variable.
- x1,x2,…,xnx_1, x_2, \ldots, x_nx1,x2,…,xn are the independent variables.

- β_0 is the intercept.
- $\beta_1, \beta_2, \ldots, \beta_n$ are the coefficients of the independent variables.
- ϵ is the error term.

1.3. Types of Linear Regression

1. **Simple Linear Regression**: Involves a single independent variable and models the relationship between the dependent and independent variable with a straight line.

2. **Multiple Linear Regression**: Involves multiple independent variables and models the relationship with a hyperplane in multi-dimensional space.

1.4. Implementation Steps

1. **Data Preparation**:
   - **Feature Selection**: Choose relevant features that have a significant impact on the target variable.
   - **Data Cleaning**: Handle missing values, outliers, and ensure data is in a suitable format.

2. **Model Training**:
   - **Split Data**: Divide data into training and testing sets to evaluate the model's performance.
   - **Fit Model**: Use algorithms like Ordinary Least Squares (OLS) to fit the linear model to the training data.

3. **Model Evaluation**:

- **Metrics**: Evaluate model performance using metrics like Mean Absolute Error (MAE), Mean Squared Error (MSE), and R-squared.
- **Residual Analysis**: Check residuals (differences between observed and predicted values) to assess model fit.

4. Implementation in Python:

```python
Code
from sklearn.linear_model import LinearRegression
from sklearn.model_selection import train_test_split
from sklearn.metrics import mean_squared_error

# Load data
X = # feature matrix
y = # target variable

# Split data
X_train, X_test, y_train, y_test = train_test_split(X, y, test_size=0.2, random_state=42)

# Initialize and train model
model = LinearRegression()
model.fit(X_train, y_train)
```

```
# Make predictions
y_pred = model.predict(X_test)

# Evaluate model
mse = mean_squared_error(y_test, y_pred)
print(f'Mean Squared Error: {mse}')
```

1.5. Use Cases

- **Predicting House Prices**: Estimating property values based on features like size, location, and number of rooms.
- **Sales Forecasting**: Predicting future sales based on historical data and marketing spend.

1.6. Best Practices

- **Feature Scaling**: Standardize or normalize features to improve model performance, especially when features vary in scale.
- **Regularization**: Use techniques like Lasso or Ridge regression to prevent overfitting and handle multicollinearity.

2. CatBoost

2.1. Overview

CatBoost (Categorical Boosting) is a gradient boosting library developed by Yandex. It is specifically designed to handle categorical features effectively and performs well on a variety of data types.

2.2. Key Features

1. **Handling Categorical Features**: CatBoost natively supports categorical features without the need for extensive preprocessing.
2. **Efficient Training**: Uses advanced techniques to reduce training time and memory usage.
3. **Robustness**: Provides strong performance even with noisy or missing data.

2.3. Mathematical Foundation

CatBoost is a variant of gradient boosting that builds an ensemble of decision trees to improve prediction accuracy. It optimizes the model by minimizing a loss function through iterative boosting.

2.4. Implementation Steps

1. **Data Preparation**:
    - **Categorical Encoding**: Although CatBoost can handle categorical features directly, ensure features are correctly identified.
    - **Data Splitting**: Divide data into training and validation sets.
2. **Model Training**:
    - **Initialize Model**: Set up CatBoost parameters, including learning rate, depth of trees, and number of iterations.
    - **Train Model**: Fit the CatBoost model to the training data.
3. **Model Evaluation**:

- **Metrics**: Evaluate using metrics such as accuracy, AUC (Area Under the Curve), and F1-score for classification tasks.
- **Feature Importance**: Assess feature importance to understand the impact of different features.

4. **Implementation in Python:**

python

Code

```python
from catboost import CatBoostClassifier
from sklearn.model_selection import train_test_split
from sklearn.metrics import accuracy_score

# Load data
X = # feature matrix
y = # target variable
cat_features = # list of categorical feature indices

# Split data
X_train, X_test, y_train, y_test = train_test_split(X, y, test_size=0.2, random_state=42)

# Initialize and train model
model = CatBoostClassifier(cat_features=cat_features, iterations=500, depth=10, learning_rate=0.1, verbose=100)
model.fit(X_train, y_train)
```

```
# Make predictions
y_pred = model.predict(X_test)

# Evaluate model
accuracy = accuracy_score(y_test, y_pred)
print(f'Accuracy: {accuracy}')
```

2.5. Use Cases

- **Customer Segmentation**: Classifying customers into different segments based on purchase behavior.
- **Fraud Detection**: Identifying fraudulent transactions in financial systems.

2.6. Best Practices

- **Hyperparameter Tuning**: Optimize hyperparameters using techniques like grid search or random search to improve model performance.
- **Cross-Validation**: Use cross-validation to ensure the model generalizes well to unseen data.

3. Neural Networks

3.1. Overview

Neural Networks are a class of algorithms inspired by the human brain's structure and functioning. They are capable of learning complex patterns and representations from data, making them suitable for a wide range of tasks.

3.2. Key Concepts

1. **Neurons**: Basic units of neural networks that receive inputs, apply weights, and produce outputs.
2. **Layers**: Neural networks are composed of layers, including input layers, hidden layers, and output layers.
3. **Activation Functions**: Functions like ReLU (Rectified Linear Unit), Sigmoid, and Tanh that introduce non-linearity into the model.

3.3. Types of Neural Networks

1. **Feedforward Neural Networks (FNN)**: Basic neural networks where connections between nodes do not form cycles. Used for simple tasks like classification and regression.
2. **Convolutional Neural Networks (CNN)**: Specialized neural networks designed for processing structured grid data like images. They use convolutional layers to automatically learn spatial hierarchies.
3. **Recurrent Neural Networks (RNN)**: Designed for sequential data such as time series or natural language. They use feedback connections to handle temporal dependencies.

3.4. Implementation Steps

1. **Data Preparation**:
    - **Preprocessing**: Normalize or standardize data, handle missing values, and encode categorical features.
    - **Data Splitting**: Divide data into training, validation, and test sets.
2. **Model Building**:

- **Define Architecture:** Specify the number of layers, type of layers (e.g., Dense, Convolutional, LSTM), and activation functions.
- **Compile Model:** Choose an optimizer (e.g., Adam, SGD), loss function, and evaluation metrics.

3. **Model Training:**
   - **Fit Model:** Train the model using the training data and validate it using the validation set.
   - **Tune Hyperparameters:** Adjust parameters such as learning rate, batch size, and number of epochs to improve performance.

4. **Model Evaluation:**
   - **Metrics:** Use metrics like accuracy, precision, recall, and F1-score for classification tasks, and mean squared error (MSE) for regression tasks.
   - **Overfitting and Regularization:** Monitor for overfitting and apply regularization techniques like dropout or L2 regularization if needed.

5. **Implementation in Python:**

python

Code

```python
from tensorflow.keras.models import Sequential
from tensorflow.keras.layers import Dense
from tensorflow.keras.optimizers import Adam
```

```python
from sklearn.model_selection import train_test_split
from sklearn.metrics import accuracy_score

# Load data
X = # feature matrix
y = # target variable

# Split data
X_train, X_test, y_train, y_test = train_test_split(X, y, test_size=0.2, random_state=42)

# Define model
model = Sequential([
    Dense(64, activation='relu', input_shape=(X_train.shape[1],)),
    Dense(32, activation='relu'),
    Dense(1, activation='sigmoid')  # for binary classification
])

# Compile model
model.compile(optimizer=Adam(), loss='binary_crossentropy', metrics=['accuracy'])

# Train model
```

```
model.fit(X_train, y_train, epochs=10, batch_size=32, validation_split=0.2)

# Evaluate model
y_pred = model.predict(X_test)
accuracy = accuracy_score(y_test, (y_pred > 0.5).astype(int))
print(f'Accuracy: {accuracy}')
```

3.5. Use Cases

- **Image Classification**: Identifying objects or patterns in images.
- **Natural Language Processing**: Tasks such as text classification, sentiment analysis, and machine translation.
- **Time Series Forecasting**: Predicting future values based on past observations.

3.6. Best Practices

- **Model Architecture**: Choose appropriate architecture based on the problem domain (e.g., CNNs for image data, RNNs for sequential data).
- **Regularization**: Apply techniques like dropout, early stopping, and weight decay to prevent overfitting.
- **Hyperparameter Tuning**: Use grid search or Bayesian optimization to find the best hyperparameters.

Conclusion

Linear Regression, CatBoost, and Neural Networks represent a range of machine learning algorithms, each suited to different types of tasks and data. Linear Regression provides a straightforward approach to regression problems, CatBoost offers powerful gradient boosting capabilities with advanced categorical handling, and Neural Networks offer flexibility and robustness for complex data patterns.

Understanding these algorithms' fundamentals, implementations, and best practices allows practitioners to choose and apply the most appropriate methods for their specific problems, leading to more effective and accurate models. Whether you're dealing with simple regression tasks, complex classification problems, or advanced data processing, mastering these algorithms is essential for success in the field of machine learning.

This detailed guide covers the essential aspects of each algorithm, their use cases, and practical implementation tips. Mastery of these concepts and techniques is crucial for building effective and accurate machine learning models.

Frameworks and Libraries for Machine Learning and Data Science

In the modern data science and machine learning landscape, various frameworks and libraries are available to streamline and enhance the development process. Understanding these tools and their functionalities is crucial for efficiently building, training, and deploying models, as well as for managing and visualizing data. This guide explores the most widely used frameworks and libraries, including TensorFlow, Keras, PyTorch, Scikit-learn, Pandas, NumPy, Matplotlib, PowerBI, and Streamlit.

1. TensorFlow

1.1. Overview

TensorFlow is an open-source deep learning framework developed by Google. It provides a comprehensive ecosystem for building and deploying machine learning models, particularly deep neural networks. TensorFlow is known for its scalability, flexibility, and support for a wide range of machine learning tasks.

1.2. Key Features

- **Computation Graphs**: TensorFlow uses computation graphs to represent and execute complex mathematical operations efficiently.

- **Keras Integration**: TensorFlow integrates with Keras, a high-level API for easier model building and training.
- **Multi-GPU and TPU Support**: TensorFlow supports distributed computing with multiple GPUs and TPUs for faster training.

1.3. Core Components

1. **TensorFlow Core**: The low-level API for building and managing TensorFlow graphs and sessions.
2. **Keras**: A high-level API for building and training deep learning models with an easy-to-use interface.
3. **TensorFlow Extended (TFX)**: A platform for deploying production-ready machine learning pipelines.
4. **TensorFlow Lite**: A lightweight solution for deploying models on mobile and edge devices.
5. **TensorFlow.js**: A JavaScript library for training and deploying models in the browser or on Node.js.

1.4. Example Usage

Building a Simple Neural Network with TensorFlow:

python

Code

```
import tensorflow as tf
from tensorflow.keras.models import Sequential
from tensorflow.keras.layers import Dense

# Load and preprocess data
```

```python
(X_train, y_train), (X_test, y_test) = tf.keras.datasets.mnist.load_data()
X_train = X_train.reshape(-1, 28 * 28) / 255.0
X_test = X_test.reshape(-1, 28 * 28) / 255.0

# Build the model
model = Sequential([
    Dense(128, activation='relu', input_shape=(784,)),
    Dense(10, activation='softmax')
])

# Compile the model
model.compile(optimizer='adam',
        loss='sparse_categorical_crossentropy',
        metrics=['accuracy'])

# Train the model
model.fit(X_train, y_train, epochs=5, validation_split=0.2)

# Evaluate the model
test_loss, test_acc = model.evaluate(X_test, y_test)
print(f'Test Accuracy: {test_acc}')
```

1.5. Use Cases

- **Image Classification**: Identifying objects in images, such as recognizing handwritten digits.
- **Natural Language Processing**: Building models for tasks like sentiment analysis or machine translation.
- **Time Series Forecasting**: Predicting future values based on historical data.

1.6. Best Practices

- **Model Checkpointing**: Save model checkpoints during training to prevent loss of progress.
- **Hyperparameter Tuning**: Use techniques like grid search or random search to find optimal hyperparameters.
- **Early Stopping**: Monitor validation loss to stop training when performance plateaus.

2. Keras

2.1. Overview

Keras is a high-level neural networks API that simplifies the process of building and training deep learning models. Initially developed as an independent library, Keras is now fully integrated into TensorFlow, providing an easy-to-use interface for TensorFlow users.

2.2. Key Features

- **User-Friendly API**: Keras offers a straightforward API for defining and training models, making it accessible to beginners.

- **Modularity**: Models in Keras are composed of modular building blocks, including layers, optimizers, and loss functions.
- **Pre-trained Models**: Provides access to various pre-trained models for transfer learning and fine-tuning.

2.3. Example Usage

Building and Training a Neural Network with Keras:

python

Code

```python
from tensorflow.keras.models import Sequential
from tensorflow.keras.layers import Dense
from tensorflow.keras.datasets import mnist

# Load and preprocess data
(X_train, y_train), (X_test, y_test) = mnist.load_data()
X_train = X_train.reshape(-1, 28 * 28) / 255.0
X_test = X_test.reshape(-1, 28 * 28) / 255.0

# Build the model
model = Sequential([
    Dense(128, activation='relu', input_shape=(784,)),
    Dense(10, activation='softmax')
])
```

```
# Compile the model
model.compile(optimizer='adam',
       loss='sparse_categorical_crossentropy',
       metrics=['accuracy'])

# Train the model
model.fit(X_train, y_train, epochs=5, validation_split=0.2)

# Evaluate the model
test_loss, test_acc = model.evaluate(X_test, y_test)
print(f'Test Accuracy: {test_acc}')
```

2.4. Use Cases

- **Rapid Prototyping**: Quickly build and test deep learning models.
- **Transfer Learning**: Fine-tune pre-trained models for specific tasks.

2.5. Best Practices

- **Modular Design**: Utilize Keras' modularity to create complex models by stacking layers.
- **Data Augmentation**: Apply data augmentation techniques to improve model generalization.

3. PyTorch

3.1. Overview

PyTorch is an open-source deep learning framework developed by Facebook's AI Research lab. It provides a flexible and dynamic approach to building and training neural networks, making it popular among researchers and practitioners.

3.2. Key Features

- **Dynamic Computation Graphs**: PyTorch uses dynamic computation graphs (eager execution), allowing for more flexibility in model development.
- **Integration with Python**: PyTorch integrates seamlessly with Python, providing a more intuitive coding experience.
- **Automatic Differentiation**: Uses Autograd for automatic differentiation, simplifying the process of backpropagation.

3.3. Example Usage

Building and Training a Neural Network with PyTorch:

python

Code

```python
import torch
import torch.nn as nn
import torch.optim as optim
from torchvision import datasets, transforms

# Data preprocessing
transform = transforms.Compose([transforms.ToTensor(), transforms.Normalize((0.5,), (0.5,))])
```

```python
train_loader = torch.utils.data.DataLoader(datasets.MNIST('.', train=True, download=True, transform=transform),
                                            batch_size=64, shuffle=True)

# Define the model
class SimpleNN(nn.Module):
    def __init__(self):
        super(SimpleNN, self).__init__()
        self.fc1 = nn.Linear(28 * 28, 128)
        self.fc2 = nn.Linear(128, 10)

    def forward(self, x):
        x = x.view(-1, 28 * 28)
        x = torch.relu(self.fc1(x))
        x = self.fc2(x)
        return x

model = SimpleNN()
criterion = nn.CrossEntropyLoss()
optimizer = optim.Adam(model.parameters(), lr=0.001)

# Training the model
for epoch in range(5):
    for data, target in train_loader:
```

```
optimizer.zero_grad()
output = model(data)
loss = criterion(output, target)
loss.backward()
optimizer.step()
print(f'Epoch {epoch+1}: Loss = {loss.item()}')
```

Evaluation code would follow

3.4. Use Cases

- **Research and Development**: Ideal for research due to its dynamic nature and extensive support for custom operations.
- **Computer Vision**: Used for tasks like object detection and image segmentation.

3.5. Best Practices

- **Use GPU Acceleration**: Leverage PyTorch's support for CUDA to accelerate training on GPUs.
- **Model Checkpointing**: Save model checkpoints during training to resume from a specific point if needed.

4. Scikit-learn

4.1. Overview

Scikit-learn is a widely used library for traditional machine learning algorithms and preprocessing in Python. It provides a range of tools for classification, regression, clustering, and dimensionality reduction.

4.2. Key Features

- **Wide Range of Algorithms**: Includes algorithms for classification, regression, clustering, and more.
- **Preprocessing**: Offers functions for data preprocessing, including scaling, encoding, and feature selection.
- **Model Evaluation**: Provides metrics and tools for model evaluation and selection.

4.3. Example Usage

Building and Evaluating a Classification Model with Scikit-learn:

python

Code

```
from sklearn.datasets import load_iris
from sklearn.model_selection import train_test_split
from sklearn.ensemble import RandomForestClassifier
from sklearn.metrics import accuracy_score

# Load and split data
data = load_iris()
X = data.data
y = data.target
X_train, X_test, y_train, y_test = train_test_split(X, y, test_size=0.2, random_state=42)

# Initialize and train the model
model = RandomForestClassifier(n_estimators=100)
```

```
model.fit(X_train, y_train)

# Make predictions and evaluate the model
y_pred = model.predict(X_test)
accuracy = accuracy_score(y_test, y_pred)
print(f'Accuracy: {accuracy}')
```

4.4. Use Cases

- **Preprocessing**: Transforming and preparing data for machine learning models.
- **Model Selection**: Comparing and selecting the best model for a given task.

4.5. Best Practices

- **Feature Engineering**: Use feature selection and transformation techniques to improve model performance.
- **Cross-Validation**: Utilize cross-validation to assess model performance on different subsets of the data.

5. Pandas

5.1. Overview

Pandas is a powerful library for data manipulation and analysis in Python. It provides data structures and functions to efficiently handle and analyze structured data.

5.2. Key Features

- **DataFrames**: Two-dimensional, size-mutable, and heterogeneous data structures with labeled axes (rows and columns).

- **Data Manipulation**: Functions for data cleaning, merging, reshaping, and aggregation.
- **Handling Missing Data**: Tools for identifying and filling or dropping missing values.

5.3. Example Usage

Data Manipulation with Pandas:

python

Code

```python
import pandas as pd

# Load data
df = pd.read_csv('data.csv')

# Data exploration
print(df.head())
print(df.describe())

# Data manipulation
df['new_column'] = df['existing_column'] * 2
filtered_df = df[df['column'] > 10]

# Handle missing values
df.fillna(method='ffill', inplace=True)

# Save manipulated data
```

```
df.to_csv('processed_data.csv', index=False)
```

5.4. Use Cases

- **Data Cleaning**: Preparing raw data for analysis or modeling.
- **Exploratory Data Analysis (EDA)**: Summarizing and visualizing data to understand its structure and patterns.

5.5. Best Practices

- **Efficient Data Handling**: Use vectorized operations and avoid loops for better performance.
- **Data Integrity**: Ensure data consistency and handle missing values appropriately.

6. NumPy

6.1. Overview

NumPy is a fundamental library for numerical computations in Python. It provides support for large, multi-dimensional arrays and matrices, along with a collection of mathematical functions to operate on these arrays.

6.2. Key Features

- **N-dimensional Arrays**: Efficient array objects that support element-wise operations and broadcasting.
- **Mathematical Functions**: Functions for linear algebra, statistical operations, and random number generation.
- **Integration**: Works seamlessly with other scientific libraries like SciPy and Pandas.

6.3. Example Usage

Array Operations with NumPy:

python

Code

```
import numpy as np

# Create arrays
a = np.array([1, 2, 3])
b = np.array([4, 5, 6])

# Array operations
sum_ab = a + b
product_ab = a * b

# Statistical operations
mean_a = np.mean(a)
std_b = np.std(b)

print(f'Sum: {sum_ab}')
print(f'Product: {product_ab}')
print(f'Mean of a: {mean_a}')
print(f'Standard Deviation of b: {std_b}')
```

6.4. Use Cases

- **Numerical Computations**: Performing complex mathematical operations on arrays.

- **Data Preparation:** Preprocessing data before feeding it into machine learning models.

6.5. Best Practices

- **Vectorization:** Utilize NumPy's vectorized operations for efficiency.
- **Memory Management:** Be mindful of array sizes to avoid memory issues.

7. Matplotlib

7.1. Overview

Matplotlib is a widely used library for creating static, animated, and interactive visualizations in Python. It provides a range of plotting functions to visualize data.

7.2. Key Features

- **2D Plotting:** Functions for line plots, scatter plots, bar charts, histograms, and more.
- **Customizable Plots:** Options to customize plot appearance, including colors, labels, and markers.
- **Integration:** Works well with NumPy and Pandas for data visualization.

7.3. Example Usage

Creating Plots with Matplotlib:

python

Code

```python
import matplotlib.pyplot as plt
import numpy as np
```

```
# Generate data
x = np.linspace(0, 10, 100)
y = np.sin(x)

# Create a line plot
plt.plot(x, y, label='Sine Wave')
plt.xlabel('X-axis')
plt.ylabel('Y-axis')
plt.title('Sine Wave Plot')
plt.legend()
plt.show()
```

7.4. Use Cases

- **Data Visualization**: Creating visual representations of data for analysis and communication.
- **Exploratory Data Analysis**: Visualizing data distributions and relationships.

7.5. Best Practices

- **Clear Labels**: Ensure plots have clear axis labels and titles.
- **Consistent Style**: Use consistent colors and styles for better readability.

8. PowerBI

8.1. Overview

PowerBI is a business analytics tool by Microsoft that provides interactive visualizations and business intelligence capabilities. It enables users to create dashboards and reports from various data sources.

8.2. Key Features

- **Interactive Dashboards**: Create dynamic and interactive dashboards for data visualization.
- **Data Connectivity**: Connect to various data sources, including databases, cloud services, and Excel.
- **Custom Visuals**: Use and create custom visuals to enhance data representation.

8.3. Example Usage

Creating a Report in PowerBI:

1. **Connect to Data**: Import data from sources like Excel or SQL Server.
2. **Create Visualizations**: Use drag-and-drop features to create charts, tables, and maps.
3. **Build Dashboards**: Combine visualizations into interactive dashboards.
4. **Publish and Share**: Publish reports to the PowerBI service and share them with stakeholders.

8.4. Use Cases

- **Business Intelligence**: Analyzing business performance and trends.
- **Data Reporting**: Creating reports for executive and operational decision-making.

8.5. Best Practices

- **Data Modeling**: Properly model data relationships for accurate reporting.

- **User Experience**: Design dashboards with user experience in mind, focusing on clarity and interactivity.

9. Streamlit

9.1. Overview

Streamlit is an open-source framework for creating interactive web applications for data science and machine learning. It allows users to quickly build and deploy web apps with Python.

9.2. Key Features

- **Simplicity**: Build interactive applications with minimal code using Python.
- **Integration**: Integrates with popular data science libraries like Pandas, NumPy, and TensorFlow.
- **Real-Time Updates**: Automatically update the web app with changes to the underlying data or code.

9.3. Example Usage

Building a Simple Streamlit App:

python

Code

```
import streamlit as st
import pandas as pd
import numpy as np

# Title and description
st.title('Simple Streamlit App')
```

```
st.write('This is a simple example of a Streamlit app.')

# Create a DataFrame
data = pd.DataFrame({
    'x': np.arange(1, 10),
    'y': np.random.randn(9)
})

# Display the DataFrame
st.write(data)

# Create a line chart
st.line_chart(data.set_index('x'))
```

9.4. Use Cases

- **Interactive Data Exploration**: Build apps for exploring and visualizing data interactively.
- **Model Deployment**: Deploy machine learning models and create interactive interfaces for users.

9.5. Best Practices

- **User Interface**: Design intuitive and user-friendly interfaces.
- **Performance**: Optimize code and manage resource usage to ensure app responsiveness.

Conclusion

Understanding and mastering frameworks and libraries such as TensorFlow, Keras, PyTorch, Scikit-learn, Pandas, NumPy, Matplotlib, PowerBI, and Streamlit is essential for effective machine learning and data science. Each tool serves distinct purposes and offers unique features that cater to different aspects of data analysis, modeling, and visualization.

- **TensorFlow and Keras**: Ideal for building and training deep learning models with ease and flexibility.
- **PyTorch**: Offers dynamic computation graphs and is highly favored in research and development.
- **Scikit-learn**: Provides a robust set of tools for traditional machine learning tasks and preprocessing.
- **Pandas and NumPy**: Essential for data manipulation and numerical operations.
- **Matplotlib and PowerBI**: Enable effective data visualization and reporting.
- **Streamlit**: Facilitates the creation of interactive web applications for data science projects.

Mastery of these frameworks and libraries will enhance your ability to build, train, and deploy machine learning models, manage and analyze data, and create compelling visualizations and interactive applications.

Advanced Topics in Machine Learning and Data Science

In the ever-evolving field of machine learning and data science, advanced topics such as Computer Vision, Natural Language Processing (NLP), and Generative AI are pushing the boundaries of what is possible with technology. These areas of study offer sophisticated techniques and models to tackle complex problems in image and video analysis, language understanding, and intelligent system creation. This comprehensive guide will delve into each of these advanced topics, exploring their fundamental principles, key technologies, methodologies, and practical applications.

1. Computer Vision

1.1. Overview

Computer Vision is a field of artificial intelligence that enables computers to interpret and understand visual information from the world. It encompasses techniques and algorithms for processing and analyzing images and videos to extract meaningful information. Computer vision is integral to various applications, including facial recognition, object detection, and autonomous vehicles.

1.2. Key Concepts

1. **Image Classification**: Assigning a label to an entire image. For example, classifying images of animals as either cats or dogs.

2. **Object Detection**: Identifying and locating objects within an image. For instance, detecting faces in a photo and drawing bounding boxes around them.

3. **Semantic Segmentation**: Classifying each pixel in an image into predefined categories. Used in applications like autonomous driving to understand road scenes.

4. **Instance Segmentation**: Differentiating between individual objects of the same class. For example, distinguishing between multiple instances of cars in a traffic scene.

5. **Pose Estimation**: Determining the pose of objects or people in an image, which can be used for tracking movements or actions.

1.3. Key Technologies and Frameworks

1. **Convolutional Neural Networks (CNNs)**: The backbone of modern computer vision, CNNs are designed to automatically and adaptively learn spatial hierarchies of features from images.

Example CNN Architectures:

- **LeNet-5**: One of the earliest CNN architectures, designed for digit recognition.
- **AlexNet**: A deep CNN that won the ImageNet competition in 2012, significantly improving image classification accuracy.

- **VGGNet**: Known for its simplicity and depth, using very small (3x3) convolution filters.
- **ResNet**: Introduces residual learning with skip connections, allowing the training of very deep networks.

2. **Transfer Learning**: Leveraging pre-trained models on new tasks to save time and computational resources. Popular pre-trained models include VGG, ResNet, and Inception.

3. **YOLO (You Only Look Once)**: A state-of-the-art object detection system that provides real-time object detection by treating it as a single regression problem.

4. **OpenCV**: An open-source computer vision library with tools for image processing, feature detection, and more.

5. **TensorFlow and PyTorch**: Both provide comprehensive libraries and modules for building and training CNNs and other computer vision models.

1.4. Example Applications

1. **Facial Recognition**: Used in security systems and social media platforms to identify or verify individuals based on their facial features.

2. **Autonomous Vehicles**: Employ computer vision to understand the driving environment, including detecting pedestrians, other vehicles, and traffic signs.

3. **Medical Imaging**: Analyzing medical images to assist in diagnosing diseases or conditions, such as detecting tumors in MRI scans.

1.5. Best Practices and Challenges

1. **Data Augmentation**: Enhance the diversity of training data by applying transformations such as rotation, scaling, and flipping.

2. **Model Evaluation**: Use metrics such as Intersection over Union (IoU) for object detection and pixel accuracy for segmentation tasks.

3. **Handling Variability**: Address challenges like variations in lighting, occlusions, and different viewpoints.

2. Natural Language Processing (NLP)

2.1. Overview

Natural Language Processing (NLP) focuses on the interaction between computers and human language. It involves the development of algorithms and models that enable machines to understand, generate, and respond to human language in a meaningful way. NLP is used in applications such as chatbots, translation services, and sentiment analysis.

2.2. Key Concepts

1. **Tokenization**: Splitting text into smaller units such as words or subwords. This is the first step in most NLP pipelines.

2. **Part-of-Speech Tagging**: Assigning parts of speech (e.g., noun, verb) to each token in a sentence.

3. **Named Entity Recognition (NER):** Identifying and classifying named entities in text, such as names of people, organizations, or locations.

4. **Sentiment Analysis:** Determining the sentiment expressed in a piece of text, such as positive, negative, or neutral.

5. **Machine Translation:** Translating text from one language to another using models trained on large bilingual corpora.

6. **Text Generation:** Creating coherent and contextually relevant text based on a given input, used in applications like automated content creation and dialogue systems.

2.3. Key Technologies and Frameworks

1. **Recurrent Neural Networks (RNNs):** Used for sequential data processing. RNNs have been largely replaced by more advanced models for many NLP tasks.

Example RNN Architectures:

- **Long Short-Term Memory (LSTM):** An RNN variant that addresses the vanishing gradient problem and captures long-range dependencies.
- **Gated Recurrent Unit (GRU):** A simplified version of LSTM with fewer parameters.

2. **Transformers:** A revolutionary architecture introduced by the "Attention Is All You Need" paper, which has become the foundation for state-of-the-art NLP models.

Notable Transformer Models:

- **BERT (Bidirectional Encoder Representations from Transformers)**: Focuses on understanding the context of words in a bidirectional manner, leading to significant improvements in various NLP tasks.

- **GPT (Generative Pre-trained Transformer)**: A model designed for text generation and understanding, with versions like GPT-2 and GPT-3 showing remarkable capabilities.

3. **spaCy**: An open-source NLP library for advanced text processing, including tokenization, parsing, and entity recognition.

4. **NLTK (Natural Language Toolkit)**: A comprehensive library for traditional NLP tasks, including tokenization, parsing, and semantic analysis.

5. **Hugging Face Transformers**: A library providing pre-trained transformer models and tools for fine-tuning and deploying them.

2.4. Example Applications

1. **Chatbots**: Using NLP models to understand and respond to user queries in natural language, enhancing customer service and user interaction.

2. **Text Summarization**: Automatically generating concise summaries of long documents or articles.

3. **Sentiment Analysis**: Analyzing customer reviews, social media posts, and other texts to gauge public sentiment.

2.5. Best Practices and Challenges

1. **Data Preprocessing**: Properly clean and preprocess text data, including removing stop words, handling punctuation, and normalizing text.
2. **Model Fine-Tuning**: Adjust pre-trained models on specific tasks to achieve better performance.
3. **Ethical Considerations**: Address issues like bias in NLP models and ensure fair and ethical use of language technologies.

3. AI Agents and Generative AI

3.1. Overview

AI Agents are systems that can autonomously perform tasks or make decisions based on their environment and objectives. Generative AI refers to models that can generate new data samples that resemble the training data, such as creating realistic images, text, or other types of content.

3.2. Key Concepts

1. **Reinforcement Learning (RL)**: A type of machine learning where agents learn to make decisions by interacting with an environment and receiving rewards or penalties. RL is used to train agents for tasks such as game playing and robotic control.
2. **Generative Adversarial Networks (GANs)**: A class of generative models that consist of two networks—the generator and the discriminator—competing against each other to create realistic data samples.

Example GAN Architectures:

- **DCGAN (Deep Convolutional GAN):** Uses convolutional layers for generating high-quality images.
- **StyleGAN:** Known for generating high-resolution and photorealistic images with controllable styles.

3. **Variational Autoencoders (VAEs):** A generative model that learns to encode data into a latent space and then decode it to generate new samples. VAEs are used for tasks like image synthesis and denoising.

4. **Multi-Agent Systems:** Systems where multiple AI agents interact with each other and their environment to achieve complex objectives. Applications include simulation and optimization problems.

3.3. Key Technologies and Frameworks

1. **OpenAI Gym:** A toolkit for developing and evaluating reinforcement learning algorithms, providing a variety of environments for training agents.

2. **Stable Baselines3:** A library for reinforcement learning that provides implementations of popular RL algorithms, such as PPO and DQN.

3. **TensorFlow Generative Models:** TensorFlow offers various tools and libraries for building and training generative models, including GANs and VAEs.

4. **PyTorch GANs**: PyTorch provides flexible frameworks for implementing GANs, including libraries like PyTorch-GAN.

3.4. Example Applications

1. **Game Playing**: Training agents to play and master games such as chess, Go, and video games using reinforcement learning.

2. **Content Generation**: Using generative models to create realistic images, music, or text content for entertainment and creative purposes.

3. **Simulations**: Developing multi-agent systems for simulating complex environments, such as traffic management or economic models.

3.5. Best Practices and Challenges

1. **Model Stability**: Ensuring stability in training generative models, as GANs can be prone to issues like mode collapse.

2. **Ethical Use**: Addressing ethical considerations in the use of generative AI, such as deepfakes and misinformation.

3. **Evaluation Metrics**: Using appropriate metrics to evaluate the performance of generative models, including Inception Score (IS) and Fréchet Inception Distance (FID).

Conclusion

The advanced topics of Computer Vision, Natural Language Processing, and Generative AI represent some of the most exciting and impactful areas of research and development in artificial intelligence. Each of these domains offers unique challenges and opportunities for innovation:

- **Computer Vision:** Enables machines to understand and interpret visual data, with applications ranging from autonomous vehicles to medical imaging.

- **NLP:** Facilitates human-computer interactions through language, driving advancements in chatbots, translation, and sentiment analysis.

- **AI Agents and Generative AI:** Push the boundaries of intelligent systems and creative content generation, with applications in gaming, simulations, and creative arts.

Mastering these advanced topics requires a deep understanding of the underlying technologies, methodologies, and best practices. By leveraging cutting-edge frameworks and continuously exploring new advancements, practitioners can drive forward the capabilities of AI and make significant contributions to the field.

Deployment and Operations: Flask and Docker

Deploying and managing applications is a crucial aspect of the machine learning and data science workflow. It involves not only deploying models but also ensuring that they run smoothly in production environments. This guide will delve into two fundamental tools in this space: Flask for building and serving web applications, and Docker for containerization and environment management. Understanding and effectively using these tools is essential for transitioning from development to production seamlessly.

1. Flask: A Lightweight Web Framework

1.1. Overview

Flask is a micro web framework written in Python. It is designed to be simple and easy to use while providing the flexibility to scale up to more complex applications. Flask is particularly popular for serving machine learning models as RESTful APIs and creating web interfaces for data science projects.

1.2. Key Features

1. **Minimalistic and Modular**: Flask comes with a minimal set of core features, allowing developers to

use only the components they need and integrate third-party libraries as required.

2. **Built-in Development Server**: Flask includes a lightweight development server for testing applications locally.

3. **Jinja2 Templating Engine**: Provides an easy way to generate HTML files dynamically and handle template rendering.

4. **RESTful API Support**: Easily set up RESTful endpoints for exposing machine learning models or services.

1.3. Setting Up a Flask Application

Basic Flask Application Structure:

python

Code

```python
from flask import Flask, request, jsonify

app = Flask(__name__)

@app.route('/')
def home():
    return "Hello, Flask!"

@app.route('/predict', methods=['POST'])
def predict():
    data = request.get_json()
    # Process data and make predictions
```

```
    prediction = some_model.predict(data)
    return jsonify({'prediction': prediction})

if __name__ == '__main__':
    app.run(debug=True)
```

Explanation:

- **Import Flask**: Import Flask and necessary modules.
- **Create App Instance**: Instantiate the Flask application.
- **Define Routes**: Define routes and their corresponding handlers.
- **Run the App**: Run the application in debug mode for development purposes.

1.4. Deploying Flask Applications

Deployment with Gunicorn: Gunicorn (Green Unicorn) is a WSGI HTTP server for Python applications. It is widely used to serve Flask applications in production.

Installation:

bash

Code

```bash
pip install gunicorn
```

Run Flask with Gunicorn:

bash

Code

```bash
gunicorn -w 4 -b 0.0.0.0:8000 app:app
```

- -w 4: Number of worker processes.
- -b 0.0.0.0:8000: Bind to all network interfaces on port 8000.
- app:app: Specifies the module and Flask application instance.

Reverse Proxy Setup with Nginx: Nginx can be used as a reverse proxy to forward requests to Gunicorn, handle HTTPS, and improve performance.

Nginx Configuration Example:

nginx

Code

```
server {
    listen 80;
    server_name yourdomain.com;

    location / {
        proxy_pass http://localhost:8000;
        proxy_set_header Host $host;
        proxy_set_header X-Real-IP $remote_addr;
        proxy_set_header X-Forwarded-For $proxy_add_x_forwarded_for;
        proxy_set_header X-Forwarded-Proto $scheme;
    }
}
```

Reload Nginx:

bash

Code

sudo nginx -s reload

1.5. Best Practices

1. **Environment Configuration**: Use environment variables to manage configuration settings and secrets.

2. **Error Handling**: Implement error handling and logging to monitor application performance and troubleshoot issues.

3. **Security**: Secure your Flask application by using HTTPS, validating inputs, and protecting against common web vulnerabilities.

2. Docker: Containerization for Consistency and Scalability

2.1. Overview

Docker is a platform for developing, shipping, and running applications inside containers. Containers package an application and its dependencies into a single unit that runs consistently across different environments. Docker simplifies deployment and scaling by providing isolated environments for applications.

2.2. Key Concepts

1. **Images**: A Docker image is a read-only template that contains the application code, libraries, and dependencies required to run an application.

2. **Containers**: A container is a running instance of a Docker image. Containers are isolated from each other and the host system.
3. **Dockerfile**: A text file with instructions to build a Docker image. It specifies the base image, installation steps, and configuration.
4. **Docker Compose**: A tool for defining and running multi-container Docker applications using a docker-compose.yml file.

2.3. Creating a Docker Image

Dockerfile Example:

dockerfile

Code

```
# Use the official Python image from the Docker Hub
FROM python:3.8-slim

# Set the working directory in the container
WORKDIR /app

# Copy the requirements file and install dependencies
COPY requirements.txt requirements.txt
RUN pip install -r requirements.txt

# Copy the rest of the application code
COPY . .
```

```
# Expose port 5000 for the Flask application
EXPOSE 5000

# Define the command to run the application
CMD ["python", "app.py"]
```

Build the Docker Image:

bash

Code

```
docker build -t my-flask-app .
```

Explanation:

- **FROM:** Specifies the base image.
- **WORKDIR:** Sets the working directory.
- **COPY:** Copies files into the container.
- **RUN:** Executes commands to install dependencies.
- **EXPOSE:** Exposes a port for the application.
- **CMD:** Specifies the command to run the application.

2.4. Running Docker Containers

Run the Docker Container:

bash

Code

```
docker run -p 5000:5000 my-flask-app
```

- **-p 5000:5000:** Maps port 5000 of the container to port 5000 on the host.

View Running Containers:

bash

Code

docker ps

Stop a Container:

bash

Code

docker stop <container_id>

2.5. Using Docker Compose

docker-compose.yml Example:

yaml

Code

```yaml
version: '3'
services:
  web:
    image: my-flask-app
    ports:
      - "5000:5000"
    environment:
      - FLASK_ENV=production
```

Start Services with Docker Compose:

bash

Code

docker-compose up

Stop Services:

bash

Code

docker-compose down

2.6. Best Practices

1. **Image Optimization:** Use smaller base images and minimize the number of layers to reduce image size and build times.

2. **Container Security:** Implement security best practices, such as running containers with non-root users and scanning images for vulnerabilities.

3. **Resource Management:** Monitor and manage container resource usage to ensure optimal performance and avoid resource contention.

3. Integrating Flask with Docker

Combining Flask and Docker provides a robust solution for deploying and managing web applications. Docker can encapsulate a Flask application and its dependencies, ensuring that it runs consistently across various environments.

Steps for Integration:

1. **Develop the Flask Application:** Create and test the Flask application locally.

2. **Create a Dockerfile:** Write a Dockerfile to build an image of the Flask application.

3. **Build and Run the Docker Container:** Build the Docker image and run the container to test the deployment.

4. **Deploy and Scale**: Deploy the Docker container to a production environment and scale as needed using Docker Compose or orchestration tools like Kubernetes.

Example Deployment Workflow:

1. **Write Flask Application**: Develop the application and test it locally.

2. **Dockerize**: Create a Dockerfile and build the Docker image.

3. **Test Locally**: Run the Docker container locally to ensure it works as expected.

4. **Deploy to Production**: Use Docker Compose or other orchestration tools to deploy the application in a production environment.

5. **Monitor and Scale**: Monitor the application's performance and scale as needed to handle traffic and load.

Conclusion

Deploying and managing machine learning and data science applications effectively requires a deep understanding of tools and technologies that facilitate smooth transitions from development to production. Flask and Docker are integral components of this process, providing powerful solutions for building, serving, and managing applications.

- **Flask**: A flexible and lightweight framework for developing and serving web applications, ideal for creating APIs and web interfaces for machine learning models.

- **Docker**: A robust platform for containerization, enabling consistent and scalable deployment of applications across various environments.

Mastering Flask and Docker empowers developers to build, deploy, and manage applications efficiently, ensuring that they run reliably and effectively in production settings. By following best practices and leveraging these tools, you can streamline the deployment process, enhance application performance, and achieve seamless operational management.